Get

Organized

GOD'S WAY

Get Organized GOD'S WAY

Bring God's Order into Every Area of Your Life

BIBLE STUDY + DECLUTTER WORKBOOK

Eileen Koff

CERTIFIED PROFESSIONAL ORGANIZER

REDEMPTION PRESS

Published by Redemption Press, PO Box 427, Enumclaw, WA 98022.
Toll-Free (844) 2REDEEM (273-3336)

Redemption Press is honored to present this title in partnership with the author. The views expressed or implied in this work are those of the author. Redemption Press provides our imprint seal representing design excellence, creative content, and high-quality production.

The author has tried to recreate events, locales, and conversations from memories of them. In order to maintain their anonymity, in some instances the names of individuals, some identifying characteristics, and some details may have been changed, such as physical properties, occupations, and places of residence.

Unless otherwise indicated, all Scripture quotations are from the Holy Bible, New International Version®, NIV®. Copyright © 1973, 1978, 1984, 2011 by Biblica, Inc.™ Used by permission of Zondervan. All rights reserved worldwide. www.zondervan.com. The "NIV" and "New International Version" are trademarks registered in the United States Patent and Trademark Office by Biblica, Inc.™

Scripture quotations marked (ESV) are from The ESV® Bible (The Holy Bible, English Standard Version®), copyright © 2001 by Crossway, a publishing ministry of Good News Publishers. Used by permission. All rights reserved.

Scripture quotations marked (KJV) are from the King James Version, public domain.

Scripture quotations marked (NKJV) are from the New King James Version®. Copyright © 1982 by Thomas Nelson. Used by permission. All rights reserved.

Scripture quotations marked (NLT) are from the Holy Bible, New Living Translation, copyright ©1996, 2004, 2015 by Tyndale House Foundation. Used by permission of Tyndale House Publishers, Carol Stream, Illinois 60188. All rights reserved.

Scripture quotations marked (NASB) are from the (NASB®) New American Standard Bible®, Copyright © 1960, 1971, 1977, 1995, 2020 by The Lockman Foundation. Used by permission. All rights reserved. www.lockman.org.

Scripture quotations marked (GNT) are from the Good News Translation in Today's English Version- Second Edition Copyright © 1992 by American Bible Society. Used by Permission.

Scripture quotations marked (MSG) are from THE MESSAGE, copyright © 1993, 2002, 2018 by Eugene H. Peterson. Used by permission of NavPress, represented by Tyndale House Publishers. All rights reserved.

Scripture quotations marked (AMP) are from the Amplified® Bible, Copyright © 2015 by The Lockman Foundation. Used by permission. www.lockman.org.

Scripture quotations marked (NTME) are from the New Testament in Modern English by J.B Phillips copyright © 1960, 1972 J. B. Phillips. Administered by The Archbishops' Council of the Church of England. Used by Permission.

ISBN 13: 978-1-64645-585-0 (Paperback)
978-1-64645-584-3 (ePub)

Library of Congress Catalog Card Number: 2022914334

Contents

Preface

With the abundance of organizing books out there, I used to wonder why anyone would have a hard time figuring out how to get organized. However, after being in the profession for over two decades, I have come to the conclusion that what we believe dictates what we do. Therefore, some might ask, "Is clutter really a faith issue?" We believe that God desires intimacy in our daily life, but how does that translate to the clutter that sits on our tables, countertops, and in our storage spaces? This study is designed to teach you how to deal with clutter and find a peaceful place where you can nurture intimacy with God.

There are a million reasons why people can't seem to deal with the overload in their lives. That overload can be stuff, activities, or the mental perception of time. My clients have expressed that "cluttered brains equal cluttered rooms." Does God have anything to say in this regard? Is there anything in the Bible that tells us how to finally—once and for all—deal with our internal and external clutter? As a Christian Certified Professional Organizer, I say *yes*—a million times *yes*! God has shown me through His Word many passages that can be applied to living an orderly life.

It's my desire that this study will not only show you what God has to say about living an orderly life but that you can be "transformed by the renewing of your mind." Saying goodbye to clutter once and for all is my goal for you. The first several chapters of this workbook will explore why clutter (both physical and mental) creates distance between those closest to you and in your relationship with God. If we agree that God desires intimacy with us—every single day—then how does the clutter in our lives separate us from the abundant life God has provided? Your clutter could be an obstacle that keeps you from greater intimacy.

The remaining chapters will provide you with a practical blueprint of organizing how-tos for your unique situation. Looking at God's Word throughout the chapters will ensure that the Holy Spirit will lead you each step of the way.

Because I have written this in a study format, it lends itself perfectly to small groups or expanded study. Upon completion of this study, you may desire to bring this to your home church. To facilitate community change, I have devised a *Leader's Guide* to equip you in teaching this study. You can learn more at www.EileenKoffMinistries.com.

May our Lord richly bless you as He leads you into all truth!

Introduction

"I feel buried under all this stuff."

"I'm suffocating in this room."

"I'm too paralyzed to begin sorting through this mess."

Maybe you can relate to the voices I hear most every day when my phone rings or I get emails from people desperate to lead a more organized life. There are millions of people just like you who just don't know how to begin or how to make their organizing attempts last longer than two weeks.

I frequently hear:

- "I have a very hard time letting go of things, so I just keep everything."
- "My sleep suffers because I feel like I've forgotten something important."
- "I keep getting organized, but stuff just keeps coming back like a boomerang."
- "Every time I open the closet door, something comes crashing on top of me!"
- "I'd cook for my family if I could just find enough surfaces in the kitchen."
- "I'm too embarrassed to have people over to visit."
- "Just looking at this mess makes me tired and exhausted."
- "My desk and computer areas are so cluttered that I lose important mailings and information."
- "How come my office is so organized, but my home is just a pile of junk?"
- "No one in my home will help me keep things organized."
- "I'm just plain tired of always being late and never finding my keys."
- "The only order in my house is takeout!"

Do any of these comments sound familiar?

Anyone who has ever tried to get organized knows it can be tough, and that's why I have put together this study. Unlike other books filled with hints, tips, and methods that work for everyone else but you, this study will reveal God's plan for living an orderly life. Once you understand how to *Get Organized God's Way*, He will light your path to a new freedom from your present chaos. I will be sharing from my personal and professional years of experience of working with people just like you who have become successful at getting their lives in order.

Over the past several decades, the media has paid an increasing amount of attention to the world of organization. In fact, since 2001 (post 9/11), you would be hard-pressed to pick up any women's magazine and not find the word *organization* somewhere on the front cover. Since people can no longer control the chaos of the world, they have decided to at least control their homes.

Past and present TV shows highlighting a fascination with lives of excess continue to be highly rated: *Hot Mess House, A Slob Comes Clean, Clean House, Buried Alive,* and *Hoarders*. It's obvious that our culture is focused on the need for organization.

An elusive picture-perfect home is *not* the definition of a well-organized space. Organizing is not about perfection; it's about giving you access to the things you love and time to enjoy them. Others are misled when they believe that once their spaces are organized, they have achieved their goals. A well-organized space is but one piece of the puzzle that will allow you to *achieve* your goals. Here is one client's story to illustrate this point.

> *Organizing is not about perfection; it's about giving you access to the things you love and time to enjoy them.*

My client dreamed of becoming a baker, but all his countertops were so buried with clutter that he could barely bake. Getting his kitchen streamlined didn't allow him to open his bakery, but after several months in his organized kitchen, he was able to move forward with his dream because he could now successfully develop recipes designed for the bakery.

Have you ever noticed that "getting organized" is always listed in the top ten New Year's resolutions? However, in the kingdom of God, there are other motivations for leading an orderly life. After several sessions, my Christian clients come to understand that this process is truly a faith walk.

The following are a few reasons for living an organized lifestyle. I know the Holy Spirit will show you many more as you begin your journey, but most importantly, this journey will lead you into a deeper and more intimate relationship with Christ.

1. Your relationships flourish.
2. Your ability to hear God awakens.
3. Each person has certain gifts or abilities.
4. An organized life builds character.
5. An organized life maximizes time and efficiency.
6. To be ready.

Reason #1: Your Relationships Flourish

Our relationships are front and center in all that we are and all that we do.

Luke 10:27 tells us to: "Love the Lord your God with all your heart and with all your soul and with all your strength and with all your mind"; and, "Love your neighbor as yourself."

Simply stated, a disorganized lifestyle suffocates relationships. Clutter has a way of isolating us from building and maintaining meaningful relationships. Instead of constructing a safe space, our clutter actually builds walls of isolation. We can miss the blessings of fellowship because of the shame and embarrassment a cluttered house evokes. The following testimony from Miranda (not her real name) sheds a dose of reality.

Miranda's Story

Dear Pastor,

I have to tell you how I was moved to take action after hearing your sermon "Precious Praise" from the book of Acts. One of the things you spoke on was how after being stripped, beaten, and thrown in jail, Paul and Silas *still* praised God (precious praise to God, indeed).

Another was how the first response of new believer Lydia was to show hospitality. You asked, at the 9 a.m. and twelve noon services, how many of us show hospitality by opening up our homes? There was *dead silence in both services*! Pastor, the Holy Spirit worked some serious conviction with that question. It seemed like the Holy Spirit had you "hover" over the subject of this kind of hospitality for at least ten minutes (and I wanted to slowly slide down into my chair and hide). Your question that Sunday convicted me, and the absolute silence in the sanctuary only reminded me that I am not alone.

I believe you were absolutely right when you said there are many complicated reasons for not inviting people into our homes and showing hospitality. But there is one reason that prevents many of us from showing hospitality. This very shameful, embarrassing, and overwhelming sin problem is that seven-letter word, C-L-U-T-T-E-R! I've been dealing with it, and ironically, I am the Tuesday team leader of the Keepers of God's House.

I know this is a problem for more people than we can imagine. Why else would there be so many TV shows devoted to focusing on people's clutter issues? With discernment, I've discussed the problem with others who are dealing with clutter or who know someone overpowered by it—including personal friends, church friends, members of my Keepers' team, and one of my friends from the choir. It's not an easy subject to talk about. People can easily disguise it as, "My place isn't done yet," "As soon as I get that new sofa . . .," "I don't want people in my business (or my home)," "I don't have time for company," or some other "veil." However, as you like to say: "It is what it is!"

I delight in giving, and I've shown hospitality by treating people in a warm, friendly, generous way, but lately, not by opening my home. Those times when I want to be selfish, the Holy Spirit will remind me: "If anyone has material possessions and sees a brother or sister in need but has no pity on them, how can the love of God be in that person?" (1 John 3:17)

My apartment has clutter. Not like that TV show, *Hoarding: Buried Alive* (which fascinates and can inspire me), but it wasn't in a condition where I felt comfortable inviting people over. How can you show hospitality if you don't feel comfortable because you know you don't have it together?

For me, the solution was to get help (again). I had a professional organizer work with me last year for two hours. It was expensive, and the clutter eventually returned. After hearing your sermon, I prayed and asked the Lord to lead me to a professional organizer who understands organizing from God's point of view. I was excited when I found a website called faithfulorganizers.com, an organization that connects Christian organizers with clients. But I noticed that most of the Christian organizers listed in my area just did not seem "set apart" when it came to the presentation promoting their business. They seemed like the previous organizer who came to my home. And then (thank You, Jesus!), I found one called "To the Next Level." Her caption jumped out at me:

"'Let all things be done decently and in order' (1 Corinthians 14:40). Putting God above all I do is how I conduct my life and business. I treat each client as a gift from God, bringing God's order into their home or business."

Woo-hoo! I knew I had found the organizer God wanted for me.

Pastor, I've been learning about this issue from God's perspective. For example: a disorganized lifestyle suffocates relationships (with Him and other people); it builds walls of isolation between God and us and between others and ourselves. It can put God at a distance with all the distractions the clutter creates and the temptation to love and treasure those things rather than God. Sleep can suffer as a result of clutter. (Could this be a reason for falling asleep in church? I think so!) We can miss the blessings of fellowship because of the shame and embarrassment. Did you know clutter can shout over every attempt to hear God's still, small voice? Can you imagine all of us who are not hearing His voice because of clutter?

Pastor, my apartment is not yet exactly where I want it to be, but I've set goals, and I'm excited because I'm seeing results. There's progress! I'm being held accountable to commitments, and after three (virtual) sessions of working with Eileen Koff CPO® on FaceTime, I can say that I am now comfortable enough that I have invited people over. This is as a result of following her Christ-centered principles.

Miranda eventually understood how her clutter was isolating her from others, but more importantly, that a clutter-filled home builds walls between God and us. A disorganized life can put God at a distance because of all the distractions that clutter creates and the temptation to love and treasure those things rather than God. Our clutter piles suffocate our spaces, and this prevents God from releasing blessings into our lives. For emphasis, let me state this again, our suffocated spaces prevent God from releasing blessings into our lives. If the sum of all the laws is rolled into Luke

> *A disorganized life can put God at a distance because of all the distractions that clutter creates and the temptation to love and treasure those things rather than God.*

10:27, then we must always remember the importance of maintaining and creating healthy relationships, with others and with God.

Reason #2: Your Ability to Hear God Awakens

He who is of God hears God's words. (John 8:47 NKJV)

Hearing from God is paramount to your progress as a Christian, but clutter can shout over every attempt to hear God's still, small voice. It's difficult to quiet the mind and hear from God under ordinary circumstances, but it's next to impossible to hear Him when stuff is competing for your attention.

Many of my clients have sometimes expressed that when there is too much clutter in a given space, they find it "hard to hear" or concentrate. The room takes on a certain "noise" level, so noisy that the only thing they do is flee from the space. Physical clutter creates visual "noise." Therefore, the easiest way to bring down the visual noise from your life is to remove the clutter.

My client Josh expressed it this way: "I do my best thinking in the shower. There are no distractions, and I am fully present in the moment, if only during that small window of time during the day. Somehow the water running down my back helps me clear the clutter from my head, and upon turning off the water, it seems as if I reenter the demands of the day. I have become so accustomed to the clutter around me and the noise it creates that when I clear the clutter, I feel I'm back in my shower. I can think clearer, breathe better, and I smile for no reason at all."

Creating a clutter-free environment can bring about a greater sense of peace and clarity, and when you pray in a clutter-free environment, your ability to hear God's still, small voice will astound you.

In Dotty Schmitt's book *Stand on My Shoulders: Treasure from the Secret Places of His Heart*, she writes:

> It is as we cultivate a daily time of solitude and soaking in His loving presence that the Holy Spirit opens to us the rich treasures of His heart. Outward silence is certainly easier to attain than a deep inner place of quiet and stillness. This place of inner quiet is a prerequisite to hearing the voice of God.[1]

Dotty understands that hearing His voice comes with great inner awareness. She also points out that getting "outward" silence is also a key element; they go hand in hand.

As we begin to hear His still, small voice, we will anticipate His presence daily. Our purpose for the day becomes clearer, and the abundant blessings from the Father will manifest. I could never write this statement if I had not witnessed the many testimonies from my students as I have taught my previous study, *Organize His Way*. I have come to understand this simple truth . . . a clutter-free environment allows for greater intimacy and clarity from the Father.

He who has ears to hear, let him hear. (Mark 4:9 ESV)

Reason #3: Each Person Has Certain Gifts or Abilities

There are different kinds of gifts, but the same Spirit distributes them. There are different kinds of service, but the same Lord. There are different kinds of working, but in all of them and in everyone it is the same God at work. (1 Corinthians 12:4–6)

Paul speaks about the gifts of the Spirit and says that God gives to each one individually as He wills. Therefore, we are all unique and have been given special gifts and abilities. But sadly, for many of us, they go unnoticed or underdeveloped. Why? Because the world and its ways entrap us into other pursuits—like a frantic lifestyle that keeps those dreams and abilities from being at the center of our daily lives. I know this is true because my clients begin to excel in their "gifts" *after* their time and spaces become balanced. All of a sudden, their priorities become clear.

The Bible states in Revelation 3:11 (KJV), "Hold that fast which thou hast, that no man take thy crown." Translated: "Thy crown"—the blessings that come with the gifts—is then given to someone else. Your gifts and talents can open many doors of opportunity, but you must use these talents or God will seek out someone else to do His will.

Do not look at your gifts as insignificant. Remember, if you are faithful in small responsibilities, God will bless you with greater responsibilities. We will examine this in greater detail in a later chapter. I imagine God's great smile every time we use our gifts and talents that He has given us. When a cluttered environment (mental, physical, or spiritual) restricts our full potential, then the body of Christ suffers. We are all members of the same Body, and when one part is suffering, we all do. I pray that before these chapters are completed, you will begin to see your gifts and contributions to the kingdom of God. Just *getting organized* is not the goal. When you, as a believer, enter into the discipline of an organized life, you will experience the Holy Spirit in a renewed way. *An orderly life makes room for the eternal.*

Reason #4: An Organized Life Builds Character

> For we are his workmanship, created in Christ Jesus unto good works, which God hath before ordained that we should walk in them. (Ephesians 2:10 KJV)

"Character" is the person you really are. Building Christian character is a process, much like living an orderly life. If you are always stressed because you can't find what you need, your character suffers. If you are continually late and others are always waiting for you, your character suffers. If you are financially burdened because your money habits do not conform to your income, your character suffers. Living an orderly life, like a surgeon's knife, exposes root character issues and begins to let God take control. Character provides one with a sense of direction in life. People want to be around others who are productive and authentic in their witnessing.

I am reminded of a quote from an unknown source, though frequently but wrongly attributed to St. Francis of Assisi: "Preach the Gospel at all times; if necessary, use words." Our character speaks for us in the mundane of life because character voices an authentic walk with Christ. *Our character fragrance enters before any word is uttered.* Our character will draw people to Christ or repel them. I just love the translation for 1 Corinthians 14:40 from the Institute in Basic Life Principles: "Preparing myself and my surroundings so that I will achieve the greatest efficiency."

Reason #5: An Organized Life Maximizes Time and Efficiency

> The harvest is plentiful but the workers are few. (Matthew 9:37)

People's lives are getting busier and busier, so the importance of being organized from the world's point of view is more critical now than ever before. In these end times, it is imperative that we begin to see the world as our harvest field. But how can we tend our crops if distractions and life's urgencies take precedence over God's call on our lives? The secular world understands that the more organized and efficient we are with what we've been given, the more work we can accomplish. It's no surprise that time management seminars rank number one in popularity in most corporations. Living an orderly life allows you to prioritize and streamline activities that produce the greatest results. These results put people at the forefront of our attention. God is seeking individuals to reap His harvest. When our lives reflect this readiness, then we will be in our season to reap His great harvest.

Reason #6: To Be Ready

You also must be ready, because the Son of Man will come at an hour when you do not expect him. (Luke 12:40)

We will all stand before God one day and be judged on how we managed the matters He entrusted to us. It's my heart's desire that you will hear:

Well done, good and faithful servant! You have been faithful with a few things; I will put you in charge of many things. Come and share your master's happiness! (Matthew 25:23)

Many of my clients' attitudes reflect this famous quote by Bill Watterson (creator of Calvin and Hobbes):

I believe God put me on this earth to accomplish a certain number of things. Right now, I'm so far behind that I will never die.

Clutter:

- Overstimulates our systems (visual, olfactory, tactile), causing our senses to work overtime on stimuli that aren't necessary or important.
- Draws our attention away from what our focus should be on.
- Makes it more difficult to relax, both physically and mentally.
- Constantly reminds our brains that we still have a huge to-do list.
- Causes anxiety because the idea of sorting piles is overwhelming.
- Creates feelings of guilt and embarrassment, particularly when someone drops by unexpectedly.
- Frustrates us by making it hard to find anything we need—keys, bills, checkbook, etc.

Amy's Story

I try every day to spend time with the Lord. I plan on picking up the Bible and then writing down the thoughts that have been given to me. When I do find the time, it's usually sabotaged because my eyes wander around the room, and I begin to make mental and emotional notes about what I haven't accomplished, whom I need to connect with, and where various items need to be returned to.

The clutter drowns out my peace to hear anything about what is truly important for the day. I spend hours mulling over my stuff and never clearing out the cobwebs in the brain, much less on the ceiling. I don't want to miss Jesus's words of "Well done," now that I understand that these moments of distraction are sabotaging the work He planned for my day. Praise God my eyes now see, and *slowly*, I'm being awakened to listening as my rooms are set in order and life comes back to my body as well.

Becoming ready will reveal our day-to-day priorities, and those priorities are directly reflected in what God calls our treasures. Chapter two will go into this in more depth.

On judgment day, your treasures will be illuminated. What you stored up in heaven lasts for eternity. What you stored on earth will pass away. Understanding your heart's treasures, both earthly and heavenly, is one of the goals of this study. Learning how to increase your heavenly treasures will transform the way you think and prioritize your day.

The following is taken from the Daily Devotional booklet from Bob Gass Ministries.[2]

Get a Preparation Perspective
Paul writes:

We make it our aim . . . to be well pleasing to Him. For we must all appear before the judgment seat of Christ, that each one may receive the things done in the body, according to what he has done, whether good or bad. (2 Corinthians 5:9–10 NKJV)

If you are wise, you will live each day with this truth uppermost in your mind. You'll have a preparation perspective! Think about it this way. You don't just wake up one morning and say, "I've decided to be a lawyer, or a doctor, or an accountant, etc." No, you made that decision many years earlier, and then you worked towards it. Now let's be clear, as a Christian, you're not working to earn your salvation, but to earn your reward in heaven. Salvation is the foundation you build on. In the Bible, Paul says:

> For no one can lay any foundation other than the one we already have—Jesus Christ. (1 Corinthians 3:11 NLT)

Then Paul goes on to say:

> Anyone who builds on that foundation may use a variety of materials—gold, silver, jewels, wood, hay, or straw. But on the judgment day, fire will reveal what kind of work each builder has done. The fire will show if a person's work has any value. If the work survives, that builder will receive a reward. But if the work is burned up, the builder will suffer great loss. The builder will be saved, but like someone barely escaping through a wall of flames. (1 Corinthians 3:12–15 NLT)

When you stand before Christ, you will have two options—rewards or regrets. So get a "preparation perspective."

When I initially wrote this reason in my past study, I had no idea that this one theme would become the central focus of the entire study. My students kept coming back to this quote time and time again, because the focus of organizing really has nothing to do with our existence on earth. Seeking God's order in our lives today has every impact on our eternal rewards and how we are to spend eternity.

This concept sounded a bit strange at first, but after my initial students completed the study, they shared their great joy every time a drawer, cabinet, or functioning room allowed peace to enter. It was only then that they began to see the greater picture that God had intended for their lives and for those within their home. Relationships flourished, understanding the day-to-day purpose became much, much clearer, and as each day passed, new insights were gained.

One student expressed her joy with tears, sharing how her walk with Jesus was more grounded and purposeful now that she could walk into a well-organized space.

"Well done good and faithful servant!"

What's Working and What's Not?

Note what you highlighted in the preface and introduction. This is a good indicator of your values.

What's working well?

Your space is functional when you can live, work, and relax as you want. Identify what's working to your level of expectation.

What's not working?

Take a look at your space(s). What seems to be causing you the most distress? Is it the paper piles in the kitchen? Is it the blocked doorway?

List everything that just plain bugs you. Write down the consequences too. How does this affect your finances, relationships, health, and spirituality?

Focus on one area from your list above. Accept the fact that you cannot tackle everything on your list. Prioritize based on your values, as they relate to the negative and positive consequences of getting organized. Know your *why!*

Look around at the space. What is your vision for the space? Always begin with the end in mind.

How will you plan time for chapter one?

How to Use This Study

It's my prayer that this workbook will help you eliminate clutter and transform your lifestyle. Based on my extensive professional expertise and Christian beliefs, I will not only help you focus on the "hows" of organization but also on the "whys."

For example: It might be difficult for some of you to make the transition from a home filled with clutter to a clean, well-organized living space. For others, physical clutter may not be of paramount importance, but finding the time to put God first in your busy life may mean a restructuring of your daily priorities.

I'll outline methods for solving organizational issues within your home, but most importantly, I'll teach you the biblical principles for doing so. We will look at how your belief systems influence your thoughts and how those thoughts affect your actions. By infusing God's Word into each chapter, like lighting a darkened room, you'll be able to see the root causes for your clutter and what to do about it, starting with your heart and attitudes. Each chapter will feature:

- Biblical principles and study
- A different organizing area that needs addressed in your life
- Questions for reflection
- A personal story from people struggling like you
- A practical application
- A prayer
- Organizing tips
- Resources

I also hope to dispel any of the myths, lies, and false beliefs that keep you tied to your possessions and clutter. We're going to dig a little deeper to discover how our beliefs dictate our thoughts and how our thoughts reflect our actions.

- If I change my beliefs, I will change my thoughts.
- If I change my thoughts, I will change my words.
- If I change my words, I will change my actions.
- If I change my actions, I will change my habits.
- If I change my habits, I will change my character.
- If I change my character, I can change my destiny.

It's my prayer that as you work your way through this material, God will begin to declutter your heart so that you can discover the freedom of simplicity that is in Christ . . . *Get Organized God's Way*!
—Eileen

Chapter 1
Let God Shine His Face upon You and Grant You Peace: Bringing God's Order into Your Life

The LORD bless you and keep you; the LORD make his face to shine upon you and be gracious to you; the LORD lift up his countenance upon you and give you peace.

Numbers 6:24–26 (ESV)

This well-known prayer, to Jews and Christians alike, is recited in many synagogues and churches weekly. A most amazing fact is that this prayer is the only prayer that was given to the Israelites by God Himself. As a young child, I remember listening to the rabbi recite this prayer at the end of each service. Consequently, I was very familiar with the words, but not the meaning.

Recently, I was introduced to a book called *The Priestly Prayer of the Blessing* by Warren M. Marcus. To say it was an eye-opener is an understatement. Mr. Marcus does an exhaustive study into each word and dives deep into each meaning. This book was a total confirmation that the profession I chose two-plus decades ago, as a professional organizer, was exactly the path I was born to take.

Let me explain.

My maiden name was Sheinberg, so it wasn't a stretch that my nickname from my early teenage years was "Shiny." Ask anyone why he or she called me that, besides the first part of my last name, and they would say I had a smile that lit up the room. Many years passed, and Shiny turned into Koff, but the smile remained.

In 1998, after watching a show devoted to a new profession called Professional Organizers, I knew immediately that my gifting and talents had indeed become a recognizable industry. It took me two seconds to call the national association and become a member.

Meeting like individuals at a conference gave me confidence that I was a well-qualified organizer. Helping my clients turn their chaos into calm only reinforced that this occupation brought with it something that most other professions sadly lacked: *true transformation.*

There is something very special that happens to an individual when they can say that not only does their space allow them to rest and feel calm, but that they can think more clearly, have more meaningful relationships, and find a new dimension of purpose in their everyday life. Wow! Organizing a space has incredible far-reaching results that few organizers could articulate, but most knew the same story all too well.

The Priestly Blessing

יְבָרֶכְךָ יְהוָה וְיִשְׁמְרֶךָ׃
יָאֵר יְהוָה פָּנָיו אֵלֶיךָ וִיחֻנֶּךָּ׃
יִשָּׂא יְהוָה פָּנָיו אֵלֶיךָ
וְיָשֵׂם לְךָ שָׁלוֹם׃

May God bless you and keep you.
Let God shine his face upon you,
and grant you grace.
Let God lift his face towards you
and grant you peace.

Then I read chapter thirteen from *The Priestly Prayer of the Blessing*. Marcus Warren states:

> To get started, we need to understand that in the Hebraic thought, light equates to order and darkness to chaos. Genesis 1:1–4: "In the beginning . . . God said let there be light . . . and God separated the light [order] from the darkness [chaos]." By amplifying the verses, we see that when the earth was without form, void and in the dark, there was chaos. When the Priestly Blessing is proclaimed over you, you will find that the face of God shining upon you brings order . . .
>
> The enemy of our souls loves to bring confusion. As the enemy attacks us with circumstances, trials, and challenges, we often find ourselves embroiled in conflicting thoughts . . . Many times, we are conflicted and puzzled

when making decisions. Yet, when the face of God begins to shine upon us, we sense that everything is going to be okay. Suddenly we become single-minded . . . When the light of His face begins to shine upon you, He brings order into your life. Chaos, wrong thinking, and conflicting thoughts must leave. Your God-given purpose; your calling becomes crystal clear.[3]

After reading these words, I rejoiced for hours, knowing that my special profession was a direct blessing to others from God. I saw in the tangible written word that the God of the universe declared that order was essential to knowing our purpose and meaning for our lives. I see this become a tangible reality every time a space is cleared of the past and hurt-filled memories are replaced with clear space and meaning.

One could say that it was a coincidence that my nickname "Shiny" was a precursor of the path I was born to take. I see it as a divine assignment. When meeting with a new client or just conversing with others, I convey that their situation is not their fault. The world and its system teach us all too well that this lifestyle is to keep us in perpetual chaos. They begin to see, with a tangible new reality, that it doesn't have to be that way. At this moment, their light begins to shine. They begin to find peace and calm and reflect on adopting new purchase practices and finding new activities that give more daily meaning.

When the face of God radiates the glory light of His presence toward you, things are transformed. Chaos is turned to Shalom—peace, completeness, wholeness.

To Think About

Let me stress again that if your environment is one of confusion and chaos, there is no judgment here. Often, I have witnessed many clients whose self-worth is centered on material goods and multiple projects to accomplish. The thinking is: the more things look disorganized, the more worthy their lives must be.

The enemy of this world has done a wonderful job keeping distractions and chaos center in our hectic and often consuming lives. The world teaches that the more we have, the more successful we are, and we will be happier when we have more things.

Another pattern of thinking that many hold dear is that when you remove their stuff, they will miss the meaning behind the object. The fallacy of this thinking is that avoiding the problem actually creates a bigger mountain, and eventually, one that seems insurmountable.

The organizing profession allows us to bring light into a darkened environment. When newly obtained order surrounds our clients' lives, then new purpose can be fulfilled. Conversely, if I had never entered my client's home, their tornado of habitual life would continue, and peace would be an elusive dream. Order brings purpose. It is the invisible light that shines as I teach how to bring these new skill sets into my clients' lives. This same thought is paralleled in the priestly prayer that God Himself gave the Israelites.

Just as God said, "Let there be light," to bring to order that which was in darkness and chaos, so too this occurs when we can spiritually see His face, because His face is the source of illumination—of light.

Or is the Hebrew word for "shine." It connotes that when the light of His face begins to shine upon you, He brings "order" into your life. Chaos, wrong thinking, and conflicting thoughts must leave.

Your God-given purpose, your calling, becomes clear. Professional organizers are called to help our clients find a better flow for one's daily life. Christian Professional Organizers go much deeper. Our purpose is to bring order to one's life so that their daily purpose according to God's will for their life is realized.

Begin with the understanding that clutter begins first in the mind, yet when His face begins to shine upon us, we sense that all is going to be okay, and His peace begins to reign. Clutter gives way to order!

Now that you understand the "or" concept for order, what areas of order do you want to establish this week?

_____

_____

What are two steps to take to begin accomplishing it?

_____

_____

Remember that taking the land slowly is not only wise, but it is biblical. Doing too much at once brings disorder and confusion back into your mindset. Making a plan with a beginning, middle, and end process is key to accomplishing order and learning new habits along the way.

Scripture Study

Read the following verses and write down what God says to you about them.

Those who are wise will shine like the brightness of the heavens, and those who lead many to righteousness, like the stars for ever and ever. (Daniel 12:3)

_____

_____

Again Jesus spoke to them, saying, "I am the light of the world. Whoever follows me will not walk in darkness, but will have the light of life." (John 8:12 ESV)

_____

_____

The light shines in the darkness, and the darkness has not overcome it. (John 1:5)

_____

_____

In the same way, let your light shine before others, that they may see your good deeds and glorify your Father in heaven. (Matthew 5:16)

_____

_____

So Jesus said to them, "The light is among you for a little while longer. Walk while you have the light, lest darkness overtake you. The one who walks in the darkness does not know where he is going." (John 12:35 ESV)

_____

_____

And I will lead the blind in a way that they do not know, in paths that they have not known I will guide them. I will turn the darkness before them into light, the rough places into level ground. These are the things I do, and I do not forsake them. (Isaiah 42:16 ESV)

_____

_____

Your eye is the lamp of your body. When your eye is healthy, your whole body is full of light, but when it is bad, your body is full of darkness. (Luke 11:34 ESV)

_____

_____

You are the light of the world. A city set on a hill cannot be hidden. Nor do people light a lamp and put it under a basket, but on a stand, and it gives light to all in the house. In the same way, let your light shine before others, so that they may see your good works and give glory to your Father who is in heaven. (Matthew 5:14–16 ESV)

And this is the judgment: the light has come into the world, and people loved the darkness rather than the light because their works were evil. For everyone who does wicked things hates the light and does not come to the light, lest his works should be exposed. But whoever does what is true comes to the light, so that it may be clearly seen that his works have been carried out in God. (John 3:19–21 ESV)

Karen's Story

It's strange but in *that* room—you know . . . the one nobody would be allowed to go into; the one I called the storage room—I always kept the blinds closed. Even when I needed to find something, when I turned on the light, my stomach would get in such a knot that I felt I needed to turn off the light and just let the light that shone through the curtains be enough, and then get out as soon as possible.

The time came when my father was dying, and I needed to find some of his critical insurance papers. I finally resolved to clear some space. Walking into the room made me nauseous, and it took great fortitude on my part to just stay in it for thirty minutes. After several unsuccessful attempts, I finally found the small briefcase that contained those important documents. I made a resolve right then and there that I would begin to clear out the clutter and reclaim this room for my own. But how?

After praying, I realized what was most needed in the room was light—practically speaking—so I could see what needed to go or what was of value. I pulled back the curtains, and as if I was pulling back the curtains in my brain, somehow, I began to shift my thinking. What was once unthinkable to let go of now seemed meaningless.

Death has a way of putting things in a new perspective. Old sweaters, hats, and memorabilia began to find a new place—the trash can! I delighted in the hours working in this room, little by little. Each day, I seemed to find a new treasure, but most were things no longer serving a need, or a memory no longer in need of holding on to.

It was almost as if God had begun to shine in the room. First the natural light, then new lights in my brain turned on as to how I wanted to spend the next few years creating a space for me! I began to get very excited about reclaiming the space, and soon, the room was cleared and bright again. All in order and all in peace.

Now I use it to create paintings and crafts to give to my family and dear friends, and the joy it creates in me is incredible. *Through death comes a new life . . .*

Thank you, Eileen, for leading me to seek God's Word in ways never before explained. Clutter is darkness, and His order brings light.

Carole's Story

When the Lord brought me back to my first love in 2012, it was like being born again, *again*. I began to feel the promptings of the Holy Spirit to write poetry. He had identified many things that I have already let go of, but when I read *Organize His Way* at this time of my life, I realized that He knew that I would be taking your class. God is so amazing!! God used you and the class in a way that helped to change the way I live. Your obedience to Him has changed my life.

Barbara Stephan: Student, *Organize His Way*

What do You see, Lord
When You look into me?
All my hidden thoughts and ways
That I'm not able to see
And so the Holy Spirit
Gently whispers to me inside:
These are the things that I identify
You must leave them all behind

It's in My opening your eyes
That you can see and then let go
Of ways that you have always walked
That lead you from Your Lord

I bring them out into My Light
Not to hurt you, but to destroy them
Your Lord's desire is for you to shine
And draw you nearer to His side

Questions for Reflection:

How does this apply in your life?

_____

_____

What prevents you from opening the blinds in your life to let the sunshine in?

_____

_____

Taking It to God

Father,

The weather outside has an effect on my moods. When it's gray and cold, I seem to just want to stay inside, and I have much less energy to do the tasks before me. Conversely, when the sun shines, my mood is lifted and I tend to smile for no particular reason. It just seems as if my purpose for the day is clearer and more enjoyable.

After reading Your Word and learning that when You "Shine Your face upon me" You are giving me that same feeling of direction and purpose to fulfill each day with joy, peace, and contentment. I had no idea until now how much Your prayer is equaled to granting me the order and peace in my life that I am now so desperately seeking. Lord, only You can lead my steps. Shine Your light upon me so I may see Your glory and feel the peace that comes when living an ordered life. Thank You, Lord, for Your revelations.

In Jesus's name, Amen.

Chapter 2
Where are Your Treasures?
Assessing Material Possessions

For where your treasure is, there your heart will be also.
Matthew 6:21

When my son Evan was a small child, he had an intense desire to own a particular LEGO set. After many months of dreaming and talking about it, his birthday finally arrived and he received his heart's desire—the new LEGO Space Station! Evan spent hours constructing and playing, but after a few weeks, the allure of the new LEGO set disappeared, and he was on to something else. That's often what happens with earthly treasures. The pleasure is temporary, leaving you always wanting something more.

It's so easy to get caught up in this materialistic world of ours, isn't it? Before we know it, the desire for that fancy new car, new home, or some other material possession dominates our hearts and minds. "Things" can begin to consume our thoughts, leading us on a pursuit of acquiring more while we push away and replace God as number one in our lives.

Before we can get into the practical how-tos of organizing our lives, we have to first examine what it is we love, what we really treasure. That will tell us a lot about our possessions and ourselves and how tightly we are holding on to the very things that often end up cluttering our lives. A treasure is not so much a physical want, but a heart's desire.

Let's take a look at the Parable of the Hidden Treasure and the Pearl of Great Price to help us out. The Bible says:

The kingdom of heaven is like a treasure hidden in a field. When a man found it, he hid it again, and then in his joy went and sold all he had and bought that field. Again, the kingdom of heaven is like a merchant looking for fine pearls. When he found one of great value, he went away and sold everything he had and bought it. (Matthew 13:44–46)

My paraphrase to the Matthew scripture would sound like this:

A treasure in heaven simply means living a life with open hearts and open hands. We must know the value of what we are searching for, and we must know where to find it.

How willing are we to trade in all our possessions in order to receive the kingdom of heaven as the man in this passage does? Upon finding the treasure in the field, he goes and sells all he has in order to buy the field so that he can own the treasure that is hidden there—a treasure so immeasurably amazing that it's worth sacrificing all in order to receive it.

Where are you investing?

_____

_____

Where are you spending?

_____

_____

What are you sacrificing?

_____

_____

The answers to these questions will be a good indicator of where your heart is. Matthew 6:19–21 says, "Do not store up for yourselves treasures on earth . . . for where your treasure is, there your heart will be also." Let's consider what Jesus means by our hearts. Jesus is speaking about the very core of our being—our emotions, wishes, and wills. What we long for and desire is our treasure, and seeking after that treasure will move our entire being to seek after it. Our hearts are like a needle of a compass, always pointing in the direction in which our treasures are kept. Our earthly treasures are kept here on earth; our heavenly treasures are kept for us when we return home.

Treasure in this context refers to a "treasure store." It's a concentration of riches, often one that is considered lost or forgotten until it's rediscovered. Just as your use of time says a lot about your priorities, so your material things (treasures) say a lot about your heart and thoughts.

To Think About

What is your treasure? Is it your house, your clothes, your possessions, or your job? Is it fame? Comfort? Belonging?

> *Our hearts are like a needle of a compass, always pointing in the direction in which our treasures are kept.*

Whatever you love—that is your god. You carry your love for it in your heart. It's something you think about day and night. He who lays up treasure for himself is not rich toward God.

We store up treasure in heaven by seeking the kingdom of God through helping others. According to Matthew Henry's *Concise Commentary on the Whole Bible:*

Christ counsels us to make our best things the joys and glories of the other world, those things not seen, which are eternal, and to place our happiness in them. There are treasures in heaven. It is our wisdom to give all diligence to make our title to eternal life sure through Jesus Christ, and to look on things here below, as not worthy to be compared with it, and to be content with nothing short of it . . . A man may do some service to two masters, but he can devote himself to the service of no more than one. God requires the whole heart, and will not share it with the world. When two masters oppose each other, no man can serve both. He who holds to the world and loves it, must despise God; he who loves God, must give up the friendship of the world.[4]

Mary's Story

I have to look at my life and what my treasures on earth really are. I choose to do so because I feel I have no choice but to get rid of the shame and disappointments my home is bringing me. I find that God reveals things to me as I declutter. My current treasures, I've discovered, are rolls and rolls of wrapping paper. Hidden in my closet was wrapping paper, intended for the holidays, but now the rolls are so badly damaged they are junk. I can no longer use them for the holidays for which they were intended.

Many holidays have gone uncelebrated. I cannot even bring friends and family into my home because of my home's condition. As a result, I am not bringing joy to other people at all. My heart remains closed in shame because I can't get my home orderly enough to celebrate, so the intended wrapping paper for past gifts haunts my memories.

What we store on earth is where our heart is, and my heart is not in the right place. I have chosen to put my heart in a pile of junk! This didn't happen overnight. It was a series of small choices I made. Satan would love for me to continue making excuses to keep this going. However, I need to be completely honest with myself and with God. I need to confess this series of "harmless" sins I have committed in choosing not to deal with "this" and "that" today. Saving unused items doesn't add to my life or my ability to serve God. Stocking up for just-in-case days keeps me chained to my past.

I need to trust that God will provide what I need so I don't have to store it up. In order to be free—to follow God and to trust Him—I need to lighten my mental, physical, and spiritual load. I can say over and over again that I want to serve God; but if I choose to enclose myself in a prison of pain and clutter, I am useless. There is no point to it and no need for it. I'm frightened to really follow God. But deep in my heart, I know that with God running the show, I know there is nothing to fear.

Lord, I need to trust You today and more every day. Speak to my heart and place trust there so that I am not afraid to truly follow You and to live the life You have purposed for me according to Your will. Lord, I believe. Forgive me and help my unbelief.

Questions for Reflection:
1. How would you define what "treasure" means to you?

_____

_____

2. Where is God in relation to what you love?

_____

_____

3. What is an earthly treasure?

_____

_____

4. Name three earthly treasures you own.

    1. _____

    2. _____

    3. _____

5. What is a heavenly treasure?

_____

_____

6. What does this treasure look like stored up for you in heaven?

_____

_____

7. How you spend your money greatly determines your priorities. Where have your priorities been this week? (Examine your checkbook, credit card statements, etc.)

_____

_____

8. Has this been a typical or atypical week?

_____

_____

9. Name three purchases you recently made and your reasons for buying them.

    1. _____

    2. _____

    3. _____

10. What treasures do you have at home?

_____

_____

11. What condition are they in?

_____

_____

12. Do you have generational/family treasures?

_____

_____

13. How do you honor and respect them?

_____

_____

14. How congruent are your treasures and your beliefs?

_____

_____

To maintain right relationships to our "earthly treasures" while laying up "treasures in heaven," we need a different perspective. The rich young ruler in Matthew 19:16–22 went away sorrowful, for he had great possessions. In spite of his longing to gain eternal life, the request to let go of his earthly possessions was just too much for him. Jesus looks at our hearts, and the lad's heart was with his treasures on earth. Do your earthly treasures hinder your ability to walk with God?

The Sock Drawer Story

During one of my classes in *Organize His Way*, I gave what I call the "sock drawer" example. One of my students in the class stated that she had a drawer bulging with all of her socks. No matter how many times she tried to organize her array of socks (white crew and sport, black, brown, tan, red, green, blue, purple, and yellow, dress, polka-dotted, toe-in, multicolored, striped, and fuzzy) they all ended up in a mess just a few days later.

As the organizing expert, I began my classic, "Have you tried this scenario?"

A dear sister in the back of the room stood up. "Why don't you just keep the essentials? The black, brown, and tan and a few favorites from the others. Let everything else go."

As she was speaking I could see the sock student's face contort with an expression of *I'd rather die than to let go of my socks.*

When I saw her face, I was reminded of the rich young ruler and Jesus's encounter. Even though the lad had kept the "law," upon hearing Jesus's instruction to sell and give, he was greatly saddened. He knew what he must do, this was a once-in-a-lifetime opportunity, but he couldn't let go of his treasures. His stuff had become his idol.

God clearly states that we shall have no other idols above Him. God never demands we change. In this story, he doesn't stop the ruler; he lets him go away, knowing how very sad he was. God will never force or change His way to accommodate us. The sock drawer can stay as full as you want it to be. You can stay frustrated with the socks of life, or you can begin to let go and experience the freedom that is in Christ.

Scripture Study

Jesus has a way of reaching down to our very core and challenging our thoughts. What are you living for?

Look up the following verses and reflect on how they might help you keep your heart focused on the *right* treasure.

Proverbs 2:4–5

_____

_____

Luke 12:33

_____

_____

Shedding What You Don't Treasure and Honoring What You Do: Eliminating Homelessness from Your Home

We've all heard the adage, "A place for everything, and everything in its place." Barbara Hemphill, CEO and founder of Productive Environment Institute, states that, "Clutter is postponed decisions®" Your piled-up stuff represents nothing more than a delayed decision to put it where it belongs. Not giving each item a home simply means that you haven't taken the time to figure out if it's important enough to keep or think about where it should go.

> *"Clutter is postponed decisions®."*

Every item in your home was brought in one at a time, so each item should have a place where it can be properly put away. For example: Every piece of paper that finds its way into your house should have a home. I know this can sound daunting, but in the chapter "Like Paper, Like Manna," I'll explain this in detail. I'll show you just how easy it is to make this a reality.

Once these decisions are made, maintenance is easy. Remember when you first learned to drive? Many new actions were required just to start the car. Now you are so accustomed to starting your car that you never have to think about it. The same will happen with eliminating clutter in your home. You *can* build a new lifestyle. In a matter of only a few months, maintaining a clutter-free home will become effortless.

The bottom line is that many of us do not have the proper space in our homes to keep all of our possessions. Quite frequently, I get calls from inquiring clients who want me to come in and organize their space, but *not get rid of anything.* Our society simply has too much stuff.

Keeping everything and not giving honor to our possessions undermines our ability to feel gratitude for them. The more you have, the less often you will feel gratitude for your possessions and the incredible things they allow you to do.[5] All of our stuff has a cost. Yes, the purchase of the item came with a price tag, but the cost of maintaining it is even greater. There are a host of psychological costs to everything we keep, especially if those things exist in a state of disorder.

Clutter just feels bad to be around. I have seen dramatic changes in the lives of my clients as a result of their ability to honor what they keep by tossing, selling, or donating what is no longer serving their present lives. Many have told me that their sleep, for example, is markedly better. They tell me that they can actually sleep longer and dream more deeply. Housecleaning no longer takes all weekend to complete and that allows them to pursue outside interests. Decluttering will not only transform your home; it will transform your life!

When speaking with a new client, I explain that clutter is not the problem. It's not about their stuff. Rather, he or she must learn to deal with the power of the object. I agree with Peter Walsh, organizing expert, when he says:

> When objects hold a tremendous amount of power over someone, then I have discovered that people lose the ability to choose which items are important. *Everything* becomes important, and if this is the case, then nothing is important. If all has equal value, if all of the baby clothes are important, and all of the art drawings are important, or if all of the craft supplies are important, what usually happens is a feeling of a lack of honor or respect for any of it! If stuff is packed away in a box to deteriorate either by age, mold, or animals, then giving honor to those items is meaningless.[6]

I start by getting my clients to tell the story of the object. For example: If among your prize possessions is an old hat once worn by your father, his watch, pictures, and letters, I will suggest to my client that we get a shadow box and arrange those items in it and display it in a room that will allow the family to see and remember Dad. Honoring the few and discarding the rest releases the client's guilt of having to save it all.

Whose Stuff Is It Anyway?

> The world and all that is in it belong to the LORD; the earth and all who live on it are his. (Psalm 24:1 GNT)

In Rick Warren's *The Purpose Driven Life,* he states:

We never really own anything during our brief stay on earth. God just loans the earth to us while we're here. It was God's property before you arrived, and God will loan it to someone else after you die. You just get to enjoy it for a while[7]

I might add that even though you may think he's speaking of property on the earth, I would suggest that *everything* in your home actually belongs to God. That coat you bought last fall is His. Remember, He gave you or your spouse the income so that you could afford the coat. He supplied all the raw materials that go into the coat, and He made the people who manufactured the coat. How it got into your hands was all *His* doing. The coat actually does belong to Him, and He loves you so much that even a coat to keep you warm in winter is important to Him.

Warren continues:

Our culture says, "If you don't own it, you won't take care of it." But Christians live by a higher standard: "Because God owns it, I must take the best care of it that I can." The Bible says, "Those who are trusted with something valuable must show they are worthy of that trust." (1 Corinthians 4:2 NCV) . . .

At the end of your life on earth, you will be evaluated and rewarded according to how well you handled what God entrusted to you. That means everything you do, even simple daily chores, has eternal implications."[8]

Whoever can be trusted with very little can also be trusted with much, and whoever is dishonest with very little will also be dishonest with much. So if you have not been trustworthy in handling worldly wealth, who will trust you with true riches? And if you have not been trustworthy with someone else's property, who will give you property of your own? (Luke 16:10–12)

In sessions with my clients, as well as presenting at speaking engagements, I am always asked these questions:
Is clutter really a *faith* issue?
Does it really matter if I let the endless to-do lists go undone?
It's hard to believe that God really cares if I hang up my coat!

I can assure you, God is concerned! Even when it comes to the smallest of details, He needs to see you can handle the small things before He entrusts you with greater responsibility. (My paraphrase for Luke 16:10–12).

It's the same story time and again—clients tell me they want to have it all, but they hesitate in taking the responsibility. So many times, I've seen my clients' homes piled high with stuff—but the family is oblivious to the negative effects the clutter has on communication and cooperation.

In every meeting I have with a client, I strive to act as God's hands and feet, shedding His love and influence into each situation. I teach my clients that when we are responsible for the way we take care of our items, then those around us begin to follow in kind.

Case in point, I was recently working with a woman whose son repeatedly neglected to straighten his own room; but when he saw how his mother and I were working together to organize the home at large, his personal habits changed as well. He had simply been waiting to see the "right thing" done so that he could incorporate the same changes. Never underestimate the smallest of actions and the impact it might have on others.

> Every action in our lives touches on some chord that will vibrate in eternity.
> —Edwin Hubbell Chapin

We must always strive to do what is honorable and just, not only with our actions, but also with the items that God has provided in each of our lives. Where we spend our time, with whom we associate, and even the purchases we make will profoundly affect our eternal rewards.

> *We must always strive to do what is honorable and just, not only with our actions, but also with the items that God has provided in each of our lives.*

In our struggle to loosen ourselves from the entangling net of clutter, we may lose sight of an important factor: it's not about us. Above all, Jesus demands we love Him more than anyone or anything. This requires us following Him, trusting Him, and being satisfied only in Him. Only then will we be able to receive and manage the true riches He desires to give us. Become faithful with the small things, and the greater *will* be added unto you.

Organizing Tips: Eliminating Homelessness from Your Home

Pray.

Let your prayer be focused on what God's desire is for your space. I've heard it said many times that our intentions are not necessarily God's intentions. We may think we need to start in room A, but during prayer, God makes it clear that we are to start in room B. Our prayers direct our paths. As you open your heart to God, He will speak to you about your clutter and each possession.

Let God shine His light on a small area of your home.

Once you have decided what is a treasure, give it the honor and respect it is due. Honor each item with a "home," where it is properly put away.

Display your treasures.

If you choose to display your honored memorabilia, you might want to consider using museum wax to anchor your items and avoid damage. Follow the preservation as suggested by museums or historical societies.

The internet is a wonderful source for instructions on how to care for almost anything. The American Institute for Conservation is a great place to find a conservator and suggestions on how to save your treasures. You can also learn much from the way experts at the Smithsonian Institution (www.smithsonian.org) take care of their great treasures. Another easy-to-use website is the Minnesota Historical Society (www.mnhs.org). Your local historical society or museum might also be a great resource, as are appraisers in your local area.

Store your items at the "point of use."

This system refers to organizing things so that they come to hand easily when they're needed. This "point of use" system allows you to easily access what you need in direct relation to how often you use it.

Most people don't have a place-for-everything-and-everything-in-its-place system, so they put things where they fit. This is why people keep an abundance of plastic shopping bags in the pantry, or in a kitchen drawer or even in a cabinet by the pots and pans. There is no logical place to put them and that's why they seem to accumulate. I've even heard that they go in the drawer under the kitchen cloths, because that's where Mom used to keep them.

The core of the point-of-use system is having a well thought out plan. Consider how you want your home to function, and remember the point-of-use rule. The following four question will help you to move toward your next steps.

Organizing Questions to Help You Get Started

How can you begin to eliminate homeless items in your home?

_____

_____

On a scale of 1 (not ready at all) to 10 (very ready), how ready are you to do this?

_____

_____

If every item in your house had a home, what would the positive outcomes be?

_____

_____

Are those outcomes important to you?

_____

_____

What consequences might you experience if you don't get started?

_____

_____

Tala's Story

I read the first chapter a couple of times because it didn't sink in. I don't have a "collection" of any sort that I could think of—I don't collect dolls or teacups or anything that would be considered a "treasure." I went through the questions and answered them as best as I could but couldn't really see how it could help me.

After praying about it, the word "treasure" stuck in my head. I would look at my piles and think "treasure." Then I realized that there is no "treasure" in that pile; it's just junk. At least, it looked like junk. Why would I keep junk in my house? Then, I realized that I treasured my house. I love my home. I thought of my kids, whom I treasure, and realized that I wouldn't want my treasures growing up around junk.

My family comes from the Philippines, and there is a large garbage dump there where very poor families live. My parents would tell me stories and songs coming from that place, and I found it very disturbing. To a lesser extreme, if I am not careful, I will turn our home into that place. I know this is overly dramatic, but the thought of it bothers me. I began to look for treasures in my house because I want my home to be a home of treasures.

Later, I began to plan my day and was watching the *Today Show*. They had a segment about clothes and trending fashions under twenty-five dollars, and I began to consider buying some things. Then, the word "treasure" popped into my head. I realized that I should not bring in "non-treasures" either. When did I start seeing my home as a place that doesn't need to be treasured—or my family, or myself, for that matter? You might not hear from me for a couple of days. I feel the urge to go through my piles of junk, and it might take a while.

How To Build Treasure in Heaven

1. Build generosity into your budget.
2. Give time and money to those in need.
3. Sell what you don't need and give the money to a hurting family.
4. Use your talents to teach others.

Barbara's Story

After reading the treasure chapter, I have come to realize what a treasure my home is. My elderly father lived with my husband and me for the last two years of his life. It was a very hard time for us as we cared for him around the clock. Life just seemed to stop, but I wouldn't change a thing because it brought me to a new phase in the Lord.

A few months after my father's passing, we decided to do some redecorating. The house had become a hospital, and we wanted to make it our own again.

We hired an interior designer, and all purchases made and work done reflect who we are today. Each piece and placement in our home is of value in my heart. But what is truly amazing is that if you came into my home, you would never think I needed help in organizing. Everything looks very neat and orderly, but don't open a closet, or drawer, or cabinet.

I have spent most of my life cleaning out, reorganizing, getting spaces to look good, only to have the cycle repeat itself over and over because I hadn't changed my ways. I see now that doing this "God's Way" is what makes the difference. I have asked God to go into every area of my heart, even the places I don't know about, and I have given Him free access to clean it all out so He can be upon the throne in my heart.

And look where He has brought me: to all the stuff and clutter behind closed doors and cabinets. Nothing is hidden from Him. I have it hidden, so everything looks neat and clean, and, although I am disgusted with this aspect of my life, I have been complacent and given up. But He sees it and wants to free me from it. So He has brought me to *Get Organized God's Way*, and He has already blessed me.

As I focus more on God's kingdom, which is eternal, I will focus less on the temporary things that I have accumulated and not let go of. I want to seek God for His wisdom and not allow my fleshy heart to be drawn away from His treasures. I want to replace my desires with His and my ways with His. As I seek Him in this and obey and make immediate right choices, my life will change, and I will honor Him.

Taking It to God

Father,

I know I'm to store up my treasures in heaven, but quite frankly, I have no idea what that means. How do I store up something I can't physically see or understand? I know You will reveal this to me as I seek Your Word and listen to Your voice. Thank You for showing me that what's in my heart has a direct correlation to what I love. Forgive me for pursuing so many earthly possessions and activities. I realize now that by doing so, I have shut the door on the blessings You had purposed for me.

I humbly confess and ask Your forgiveness for keeping these false treasures. I understand that laying up my treasures in heaven is when I give of myself to the service of others in Christ's name. I ask You to shine Your light on the treasures I need to store up in Your kingdom. Help me realize the difference between "stuff" and "treasures." Most of all, help me to always treasure You above all other treasures in my life. Amen.

Chapter 3
A Changed Mind Can Change Anything

For as he thinketh in his heart, so is he.

Proverbs 23:7 KJV

Have you ever noticed the wall of planners and calendars in your local office supply store? It seems there are hundreds of styles and sizes, each promising us an organized "twenty-five-hour" day.

I think I have seen just about every type and brand of these products in my clients' homes. In fact, if I could retrieve every unused planner/calendar that I have come into contact with, I could open up my own planner store!

Planners whisper the reality of "getting it all done." People buy products and sometimes multiple products like planners because they believe they will become their change agent. Advertisers are wizards at masking reality. They wave the product's magic wand, and we believe it's the product that will do all the work.

To Think About

How much time and energy do you spend trying to attain something, whether emotionally or physically, which you believe you need in order to be happier, more fulfilled, or make life easier? Common examples of where we can get caught up in the "chase" include:

- Believing we need someone's approval
- Believing the next "planner" will organize our lives (instead of organizing it ourselves)

- Believing that some better-than-Botox cream will make us beautiful
- Believing our child needs a specific brand item or toy to be happy . . .
- Believing the new cookware will create family dinners
- Believing we are responsible for someone else's happiness[9]

Barbara's Story

I woke one morning last week with brain fog. I sensed a real shift in my vision and thinking. I'm sure there have been days when you, too, have waddled through not knowing if you're tired, getting sick, or just emotionally spent. For whatever reason, the fog stayed with me for several days. Unable to focus or function in my daily routines, the TV became my close friend, second only to the computer.

Flipping the channels was my exercise du jour. "Oh, look, the Home Shopping Network! Wow! I never saw that before. Wow! I could really use that." Yawn. "I really need that!"

Followed by, "Hello, yes, I'd like to order . . . Why? Well, I just know that it's going to make my life easier, and I can't wait for it to get here. Ship it fast!"

Three hours later, I awoke on the couch still feeling tired and hungry, but with no motivation to move. I must feed the cat; the kids can make peanut butter and jelly sandwiches for dinner. Oh, I haven't checked my emails today.

Checking my emails, I wonder if Susan has responded to my letter. Yawn. Why can't I seem to focus? Two hours later and three hundred dollars spent on books, pots, and linens, I turn off the TV and computer.

Feelings of guilt begin to mount. Tempers begin to shorten.

As I turn from the desk, I notice that every square inch of ground is littered with something: clothes, books, laundry, papers, food wrappers, and cans. You get the picture.

"I'll deal with this tomorrow."

What a pity, you are sure to be thinking. *This poor soul is in real need of help.*

Help is right! But the shame and fear of not living up to others' standards keeps me from seeking the help I desperately need. So the cycle continues.

You may have read the following:

Watch your thoughts, for they become words. Watch your words, for they become actions. Watch your actions, for they become habits. Watch your habits, for they become character. Watch your character, for it becomes your destiny. —Attributed to Frank Outlaw

I would add, "Watch your beliefs, for they become your thoughts!"

Where your mind goes, the rest of you will follow. Thoughts determine your attitudes and perspective and, ultimately, the overall quality of your life. Your thoughts are powerful!

Scripture reminds us to be very wary with what we spend time thinking about. Paul writes in Philippians 4:8 (NLT):

And now, dear brothers and sisters, one final thing. Fix your thoughts on what is true, and honorable, and right, and pure, and lovely, and admirable. Think about things that are excellent and worthy of praise.

> *Where your mind goes, the rest of you will follow.*

Paul knew that in order to wage constructive warfare, we must take captive every thought.

In Rick Renner's book *Dressed to Kill*, he states:

The devil's entrance into the life of a believer is allowed primarily through that believer's negligence. He slips in through an uncommitted, unrenewed area of the mind—a loophole—and then begins to wage warfare against the mind and flesh of that individual.

The word Kosmokrateros (rulers of the darkness of this world) is a military term that has to do with discipline, organization, and commitment. The devil is so serious about doing damage to humanity that he deals with demon spirits as though they are troops. He puts them in rank and file and organizes them to the hilt. Yes, we do have more authority than the devil has; we do have the Greater One living in us. The Church of Jesus Christ is loaded with heaps and heaps of raw power. But at this particular time, that power is disconnected and disjointed by a Body that lacks discipline, organization, and commitment.[10]

Unless we are serious about changing our mindsets that keep us in bondage to our daily lifestyles, we remain ineffective for the kingdom of God.

Questions for Reflection:
    1. What do you think about?

_____

_____

    2. Name three things that you tend to think about during the day. Are they related to work, family, or money?

        1. _____
        2. _____
        3. _____

Understanding that our beliefs control our thinking, and that our thinking controls our actions and, ultimately, our destinies, what does the Bible say about right thinking? God's Word very clearly says that you must not *only* be born again, but that you must be continually "renewing your mind" (see Ephesians 4:22–23). This is not a one-time event, but a lifelong process. If you do not change the way you think, you will remain stuck, trapped, stifled, and unable to grow. Old thoughts, like cement, will keep you bound up, preventing you from moving forward to a clear, resilient, and creative way of living.

The pursuit of an organized life, or even a slightly more organized life, will remain elusive unless our beliefs about change are clear. Solomon offers us a powerful approach to use as we think about change: "For as he thinketh in his heart, so is he" (Proverbs 23:7 KJV).

> There can be no happiness if the things we believe in are different from the things we do. —Freya Stark

Scripture Study: The Six-Step Process for Change
    Look up the following verses and answer the questions.

Step 1: Decide to Change: A decision must be made.
1 Peter 1:13–16
What does holiness look like to you?

_____

_____

Proverbs 16:3
How can you commit this change to the Lord?

_____

_____

Ephesians 4:20–24
What are a few old ways of thinking you had before coming to Christ?

_____

_____

How have those thoughts changed?

_____

_____

What old patterns of thoughts are you still struggling with?

_____

_____

Step 2: Desire: You must want to change.
Colossians 3:1–3
In chapter two, we discussed that our heart is our mind's emotions. It's a wonderful grace process to know that God will put His desires in us. When we are attentive to hearing His voice, those desires become clearer.
What are three desires in your heart?

  1. _____

  _____

  2. _____

  _____

  3. _____

  _____

Step 3: Diligence: Stay at it, over and over again.
Diligence = discipline. Doing something over and over and over and over again creates new habits and thought processes.

Philippians 4:8–9
Name three actions you can take today to create the atmosphere of diligence in your life.

     1. _____
     2. _____
     3. _____

Step 4: Defend your mind from your old thoughts and old ways.
2 Corinthians 5:17
In your own words, name three old thoughts that keep clutter in your life. What new thoughts will replace these?

     1. _____
     _____
     2. _____
     _____
     3. _____
     _____

Ephesians 4:22–23
What is one new attitude you can apply toward your possessions?

_____

_____

Step 5: Disassociate from people, circumstances, or environments that keep you from moving forward.

Change is hard, but change done individually is next to impossible. Have you ever started on a new lifestyle eating change? Notice I didn't say "diet." Diet refers to a temporary change, not something you desire for the rest of your life.

When embarking on something that will transform your life, becoming part of a group of like-minded individuals will allow for a greater measure of success. There are many programs set up with this philosophy in mind; Weight Watchers is but one example. In community, there are shared praises and challenges, there is support, and there is a common bond. Keeping company with those that encourage and promote these newly adopted changes will give you a greater sense of encouragement and will ensure that you stay on the path longer than if you were handling it alone. That's why this is a study, not a book. It is my desire that you read *Get Organized God's Way* with your church community and draw strength from others struggling with you.

Psalm 25:4–7; 20–21

Name three people, circumstances, or environments that are keeping you from moving forward with your organization.

    1. _____

    2. _____

    3. _____

Step 6: Depend on God and God's Word for help.

Romans 9:16 and Psalm 62:7–8

Can you commit to spending time in God's Word this week?

_____

_____

Listening to God's Word in conjunction with reading the Word is very powerful. Personally, I have noticed that when I combine these two sensory elements, I can retain and absorb so much more. There are many different language apps for an audio Bible. Search out one that fits your special needs.

Write, in your own words, how this process will change the way you presently think.

_____

_____

_____

_____

How We Think Determines How We Act and Who We Become

Our inability to change keeps us stuck and our anxiety about change keeps us paralyzed in our current situations. When we address this hidden fear of change, everything in our lives opens up (even the spaces in our homes), and positive change happens much more quickly. Would you agree that what keeps us in our disorganization is our thought processes?

_____

_____

Changing our thought processes takes discipline and pushes us out of our comfort zone. However, we will never achieve our desired organization without discipline. I know we want it, but we just don't want to work on it. Many of my clients desire change but never fully realize their dream because they just don't want to give up their current way of living. Remember the rich young ruler story (Matthew 19:16–22).

Even as Christians, we can still feel separated from the Father at times because of wrong thinking. Wrong thinking will continue to keep us in bondage. There are seven elements I have found that keep most of us from changing. You may find more as the Father reveals them to you.

1. The unknown
2. What is unfamiliar
3. What is unpredictable
4. What is uncomfortable
5. What is unnecessary
6. What you cannot control
7. What may take too long

These elements keep us bound to our present habits and, ultimately, our current destiny. Wrong thinking is at the core of any disorganization issue. When I see my clients backsliding into old patterns of disorganization (which is very common in the beginning), I gently remind them that change will come when thoughts and attitudes change. The desired behavior *will* follow such change.

It is my hope that I can challenge them to begin to think in constructive new ways that lead to order. Only when these new thoughts are understood will new actions follow. These actions, diligently repeated, create the desired lifestyle.

The Importance of Right Thinking

How can we begin to respond and to successfully adapt to change that is authored by God?

According to the story in Acts 10, Peter had a vision of a sheet full of animals being lowered from heaven. A voice from heaven told Peter to kill and eat, but since the sheet contained unclean animals, Peter declined.

The command was repeated twice more, along with the voice saying, "Do not call anything impure that God has made clean" (Acts 10:15), and then the sheet was taken back to heaven.

The triple refusal here echoes the denial of Peter as described. At this point in the narrative, messengers sent from Cornelius the centurion arrive and urge Peter to go with them. He does so, and mentions the vision as he speaks to Cornelius, saying,

"But God has shown me that I should not call anyone impure or unclean" (Acts 10:28). Peter related the vision again in Acts 11:4–9. Peter first responded with pride. He might have said, "I don't need to change. Not me!" His thinking was not wrong. He was raised with Jewish traditions, and these traditions included dietary restrictions. The vision had to be repeated three times for Peter to adjust to a new way of thinking.

Change doesn't come easy at first for any of us. It takes time for us to adapt and understand why, and it may take more time than we desire. However, it is in this process that God does His transformation within us. When Peter changed his mind, he set off to Cornelius's home.

The word repentance means to "change directions." Before we change directions, we must have a change of mind. *Why change? To bring God glory—to fulfill His call on your life!*

The key to fulfilling your true calling is a right belief system, which comes from the Word of God. If it's true that actions follow what you think, then what you think is preceded by what you hold dear at your very core. Your core is reflected in your home, your business, and your life.

How Do You Break the Cycle of Wrong Thinking?

First things first. It's time to get really honest with yourself as you begin to unlearn the lifetime patterns that were created by your carnal mind, and commit to aligning yourself with the Spirit of God. How do you do that? By the renewing of your mind.

Renewing Your Mind

Romans 12:2 says:

Do not conform to the pattern of this world, but be transformed by the renewing of your mind. Then you will be able to test and approve what God's will is—his good, pleasing, and perfect will.

According to *Thayer's Greek-English Lexicon of the New Testament*, the Greek word for "renewing" used in this verse is defined as "a renewal, renovation, complete change for the better." Before any home renovating job begins, the first step is to demolish.

Personally, demo day is my favorite day of the entire process. Demolition represents the promise of something new and life-changing. To demolish our old thinking patterns, we must let God's Word tear down the false philosophies, attitudes, and actions that have infiltrated our minds to make room for God's truth.

As a demolition expert, I teach my clients how they must face their false beliefs and recognize that those beliefs have held them captive. When we demolish clutter, we demolish the prisons that have kept us in shame and embarrassment.

When we demolish clutter, we demolish the prisons that have kept us in shame and embarrassment.

One client expressed it beautifully. "The messiness of my home flows directly out of my thought processes." *Exactly the point!* "For as he thinketh in his heart, so is he."

Renewing the mind is a *daily* activity. Change is a process, not an event. When your mind is renewed you will develop a new lifestyle. Your habits become the fruit of your training.

Metamorphosis and Change

Have you ever wondered if a butterfly remembers being a caterpillar? Actually, the thought never occurred to me until I heard the question posed on a National Public Radio game show one Saturday a few years ago. The butterfly is a beautiful symbol of our "freedom in Christ," so this question held me in suspense. I often refer to this word "metamorphosis" with my clients to illustrate Romans 12:2 as they begin to let go of old habits and take up newly organized structures and systems.

Scientists at Georgetown University have discovered that butterflies do remember learned behavior as caterpillars.[11] This can parallel our own struggles. For the caterpillar, the metamorphosis process is truly a life-and-death struggle. The struggle must be accomplished entirely by the newly formed butterfly. To make this metamorphosis process even stranger, the caterpillar actually turns into a soup-like substance before its complete reforming process within the chrysalis.

All caterpillars have the genetic ability to transform, but each must go through several steps to complete the metamorphosis. What's so amazing is, if the struggle to free itself from the chrysalis is assisted by an outside force, the butterfly will never learn to fly and will lose its life. When your mind has been renewed, you will become like the butterfly instead of the caterpillar stuck on the ground, and you will have wings to soar.

As an organizer, I have seen the inner strongholds that grip many of my clients. It seems that the darkest times come just before a breakthrough, but it must be *each individual's* breakthrough. Change *is* hard. And while the butterfly does remember its former life as a caterpillar, the butterfly doesn't seem to let the past hinder its new life.

We will never forget special memories in our lives (good or bad). However, we no longer need to be chained, controlled, or hooked to the past. While my clients will not forget memories or pain associated with some objects, they need not be influenced by the memory. They can morph into a butterfly so that the chains of the past don't keep them from soaring into a bright future.

If God allowed us to go through our lives without any obstacles, it would cripple us; we wouldn't be as strong as we could have been. Not only that, just like the butterfly, we would never be able to fly. Your mind (what you believe and how you think) is truly the only territory over which you have complete control. You determine what you think about, and you determine what you do.

Remember, what you think about begins with what you believe to be true, so be sure of what you believe!

"I don't think a lot of people realize how serious decluttering is or how hard it is to change," a client once told me. "For me, it's as hard as getting rid of an alcohol or drug problem is for other people. Making these changes is not fun. I don't think I could do it without spiritual help. Every day I ask God for strength. I just wish others who struggle with this problem would realize how big of a problem it is that they are dealing with."

My client is right. After further reflection, she realized that the problem was *not* the house. She understood that the real issue was her own need for change. She realized that as her thought processes changed, slowly but surely, changes at her house would follow.

Organization Tip:

Where there is no vision, the people perish. (Proverbs 29:18 KJV)

The most important question you can ask yourself prior to any organizing job is: What is your vision for your home?

Your home is your larger self.

People, especially women, have a special personal relationship with their homes. They use it to show their tastes, interests, and personalities. The problem comes when our homes do not match who we want ourselves to be. Nonetheless, rightly or wrongly, each aspect of your home is a reflection to others of who you are. Others relate to you through what they see when they come into your home.

Your surroundings affect you too. When you live in your orderly, organized, and eventually beautiful home, you feel a sense of completeness and peace you cannot feel when you live in clutter.

One of the most satisfying parts of getting the home under control is that we are then able to creatively express who we really are in the home—both to others and ourselves.

Your first exercise in transforming your home is to visualize each space. Create a strategy that works with your lifestyle. Analyze your area before you attack. Organizing isn't just about how a space *looks*. It's about how a space *functions*. When creating a vision for your space, ask yourself what activities you will do in the space. The more activities occur in a confined area, the more clutter.

How do you want to use each room? How do want to interact in the space?

_____

_____

Now, go outside and remember the first time you saw your home. What were your dreams for the home?

_____

_____

Once you have a clear vision about the look and feel you want for your home, then you can begin to create a vision for each room.

> *Organizing is not about alphabetizing the spice rack; to define organizing is to truly uncover what is important in your life.*

One of my favorite sayings to clients is "Organizing is not about alphabetizing the spice rack; to define organizing is to truly uncover what is important in your life."

Our hectic lifestyle has a way of crowding out just what *is* important. We never seem to notice the bits and pieces of life that end up on the counter, in the drawers, and on the sofa in the day-to-day. Only when clutter becomes a nuisance, or when we decide to have others over to the house, do we then pay attention to those postponed decisions. This may result in the overwhelming feeling of how to deal with all the stuff.

Based on a true story about the famous sculptor Michelangelo, legend has it that when he finished the statue of David, a local patron of the arts, awestruck by the work, asked how he did it.

Michelangelo replied simply, "David was always there in the marble. I just took away everything that was not David."

By using a similar approach to organizing, we end up with the environment that reflects who we really are and what is truly important in our lives.

Marcus Aurelius, the wise Roman emperor, once said, "Remember this—very little is needed to make a happy life."

Look around your area. What items no longer meet the criteria for those activities? Take out everything that doesn't belong, and pretty soon, you will create an organized masterpiece!

How can you translate your vision into action steps?

_____

_____

What is the vision for the space?

_____

_____

How will you schedule the time to start organizing?

_____

_____

Do you need someone to help keep you accountable? If so, whom?

_____

_____

How many activities will you be doing in this space? Is this reasonable?

_____

_____

What does the end result look like? Keep in mind your end result. Knowing the end at your beginning will help to keep you focused and motivated.

Let's Take Action! Setting Up Your Landing/Launching Pad

Your "pad" is the first step to organizing yourself and your life, and something that simply can't wait until you have finished this workbook. Do you forget to return library books and other borrowed items on time? Do you have to go back home on a busy morning to retrieve something that was supposed to go with you? Your answer to this common problem is very simple. You need a "landing/launching pad."

Starting on the landing pad now will begin to motivate you for the rest of the weeks as you begin your organizing goals. Your landing/launching pad is a space in your home where you put things that are either "on their way in" or "on their way out." As a result, there is only one spot to look before you leave and return home. Once this becomes habit, there will be no more time wasted looking for your keys!

Here's a partial list of things to place in your designated landing/launching pad area. See which ones you need, and adapt your space using bins or furniture to hold your essentials.

- Keys
- Cell phone(s)
- Purse
- Sunglasses
- Work-related items (briefcase)
- Laptop/messenger bag
- Returns: library books, borrowed items
- Papers
- Backpacks (bins for designated area for each child)
- Errand objects
- Outerwear (for cooler or inclement weather): rain boots, snow boots, scarves, gloves, hats, etc.

Pick a high-traffic area in your home such as the mudroom or front entry. Start putting your in/out items there. Make sure the space is large enough to hold all your items easily. Then, train your family to do the same. Containing these items and then labeling the containers will remind you what is stored there. You will be able to clear your mind of all the things you once needed to remember to take with you and where they are located. Not only will you be able to relax, but you'll be amazed at how much precious morning time this saves you.

Go through the camp and tell the people, "Get your provisions ready."
Joshua 1:11a

Kathy's Story

I completed the chapter on "A Changed Mind," and I must say that I'm a bit overwhelmed. I can see why I'm cluttered. I suffer from wrong thinking, from focusing too much on flesh and earthly things. I'm caught up in the "chase" in so many ways.

I love the idea of a butterfly being able to remember its struggle and not being held back because of it, but I'm still in the cocoon and can't imagine what it would feel like to fly. I'm trying to have a vision of what my house should be and who I want to be, and all I can come up with is, "I want to be better than this."

Maybe I'm not ready. People keep telling me to not try so hard, since I have a little baby. But I know I have more to give, and what I've done in the past isn't working.

My favorite part of the chapter was the prayer: "I know there is a myriad of issues. Please shine Your light on just one." I feel like I'm standing in a storm of all of my issues and insecurities. I supposed this was internal "demolition day." I'm feeling rather exposed. Does it get better? I almost would rather stay living with my "junk" because I don't really know what it would be like without it. But if I'm focusing on God and God alone, I have no choice other than to change. I am now willing and available to make a true transformation in myself that will be reflected in my larger self, my home.

Taking It to God

Heavenly Father,

I now understand that at the core of my actions lies what I believe to be the truth about You and myself. Changes in what I believe will change my actions in terms of priorities, schedules, and monetary outlay. Father, I know that there are so many issues, so please shine a light on just one, and let's begin there. Help me to know what I truly believe, and how that is translated into my everyday life. Teach me to understand that it is not in my own efforts that these changes take place, but through Your Holy Spirit. Remind me that apart from You, I can do nothing. I am now willing and available to make a true transformation in myself that will be reflected in my larger self—my home. Amen.

Chapter 4
Keeping a Mary Heart in a Martha World: A Radical New View of Martha

But Martha was distracted by the big dinner she was preparing. . . . But the Lord said to her, "My dear Martha, you are worried and upset over all these details! There is only one thing worth being concerned about. Mary has discovered it, and it will not be taken away from her."

Luke 10:40–42 NLT

Most of my clients complain that "life happens," and even on the best days, most never seem to get it all done. I guess our perception of "all" may be unrealistic, but we live in a society that stresses an unrealistic expectation of what perfection in the home should look like. (That reminds me of the past Martha [no pun intended] Stewart shows.)

TV perfection equals being creative, well dressed, and keeping a label maker in every room. No clutter, please! This perfectionist heaven is what some of us dream about and strive to obtain. We filter through piles of facts to find the relevant ones, those that will impact our decisions. Days can often feel like a juggling act. Just when we get a rhythm, someone throws a ball into the mix. Soon, it's obvious that all the balls can't be kept in the air. I'm overwhelmed and exhausted just thinking about it!

Karen's Story

Does anyone else struggle to keep up with housework?

Right now, I am sitting in my home office. Apparently one of our puppies has decapitated a toy, and it looks like a layer of fresh snow on my carpet. My to-do list just keeps growing, and I'm getting up from my work every forty minutes to do the mountain of laundry, which six people and two dogs have created. I don't know if I should organize, clean, or take a nap.

I must say I feel a lot like whining and crying. If someone was to drop by today, I might cry. Crying is cleansing. I decided to shove it all aside and spend some quiet time with God—just ten to fifteen minutes of praying and reading the Bible. As a result, I am not only physically strengthened, but my mind has a clear directive of what needs to be done.

This is not going to be easy, but I know I am not alone. I have learned to seek first the kingdom, and then I'll know my plan for the day.

You may be asking yourself what this has to do with Mary and Martha. We are taught that Mary chooses the better priority, and that in order to apply this teaching, we need to keep a Mary heart in a Martha world. So how is this applicable in the twenty-first century?

At the end of our Scripture verse in Luke, Jesus tells Martha that Mary has chosen the better way. I often felt really bad for Martha for getting such a bad rap from Jesus. Most stories in the gospels tell of Jesus doing the miraculous, healing the sick, and preaching about the kingdom of God. This story is like a small, tucked-away, precious gift that goes unnoticed or is misunderstood.

I know I missed the point to the story for many years. Is Mary truly the better, as Jesus states? Why would Jesus tell Martha, "Mary has chosen the better way?" Someone needs to be in the kitchen, don't they? What's the matter with Martha? Doesn't Jesus understand that someone must cook, clean, and get things in order? Are not both Mary and Martha needed, and don't both have a place in the kingdom of God?

Let's examine the scene a little more closely. Jesus has accepted the invitation to have supper at the home of Mary, Martha, and Lazarus. Let's take a closer look at who Martha is. In the entire gospels, there are only four people whom Jesus loved that He mentioned by name. I'm not saying that Jesus only loves four people, but the gospels only list four by name: Martha, Mary, Lazarus, and John. That immediately helps me understand that Jesus and Martha have a very close relationship, and that Martha feels very comfortable sharing her feelings and thoughts with Him.

Because Martha has spent much time with Jesus, she sees Him as man and Messiah. In John 11:25–27, Jesus and Martha have a conversation regarding the resurrection.

Jesus asks Martha, "Whoever lives by believing in me will never die. Do you believe this?"

"Yes, Lord," she replies. "I believe that You are the Messiah, the Son of God, who has come into the world."

Martha is one of the very few that understands this man/God relationship. I can only imagine, if I were put in her shoes, how I might react every time I saw Jesus.

To continue, Scripture says that Jesus goes to their home for dinner with His disciples. This is the intimate "let's just have a simple dinner and fellowship together" meal. I can imagine Jesus needing time to just relax with beloved friends. Don't we all crave the simplicity of a meal with the loving fellowship of friends at times? One could interpret that Mary has been in the kitchen with Martha prior to Jesus' coming, and that once He arrives, she sits at His feet and shares her heart. How did Mary—a woman—position herself by sitting at His feet?

As I was writing this particular chapter, it was as if a lightning bolt jolted my misunderstanding of this scripture. I have heard this passage preached about getting our priorities straight many times, but never once did I hear it preached from the traditional biblical contextual viewpoint.

Having been raised in a conservative Jewish home, I could really relate to how this very unnoticeable and seemingly modern act could be misinterpreted. Bottom line, Mary is not supposed to be sitting with "the boys."

Isaac Bashevis Singer wrote "Yentl the Yeshiva Boy" about a rabbi's daughter whose intense desire is to be taught Torah. The young woman, Yentl, is so hungry for learning that she defies Talmudic Law by disguising herself as a man in order to attend a yeshiva, or religious school.

In biblical times, women were not to be taught by rabbis, nor could they even sit with men discussing the Torah. That is what "sitting at His feet" means. Rabbinic Judaism did not encourage intellectual initiative on the part of women. While study of the Torah was one of man's highest priorities, it was sinful for a woman to do likewise.

In the words of Rabbi Eliezer, "If any man teaches his daughter Torah, it is as though he taught her lechery".[12] Such that, "It is better that the words of the Law be burned, than that they should be given to a woman."[13]

Due to a woman's supposed lack of intellectual ability, she was also barred from the role of witness. Josephus states in his *Antiquities of the Jews* to "let not the testimony of women be admitted, on account of the levity and boldness of their sex."[14]

In modern times, Orthodox Jews allow girls to become a bat mitzvah, the female equivalent of a male bar mitzvah, but this fanfare is not on a par with the male bar mitzvah.

On *My Jewish Learning*, Erica Brown writes, "Yet in several streams of Orthodoxy or ultra-Orthodoxy, a bat mitzvah is still a nonevent. In such circles, it may sometimes be commemorated with a modest (ritual) meal, or *seudat mitzvah*, the blessing of *Shehecheyanu*, or the wearing of nicer clothes. Few rabbis in this stream of Orthodoxy would place value on a synagogue-based event, and some explicitly forbid it.[15] This rite of passage is reserved for every boy at the age of thirteen (fully twelve) to become a member of the Jewish community."

The very fact that Mary is *sitting* at Jesus' feet suggests that both Mary and Jesus are committing both a social and religious taboo. The very fact that Mary decided to step away from kitchen duties and join the "boys" in the study would have been a very radical move. Mary changed her worldview. This happened in the blink of an eye. Mary took hold of the opportunity to change her thinking, not only on the roles of women, but in a new role of influencer to those not given this opportunity.

I think Jesus was saying that Mary had boldly chosen to take hold of this offer to join Him and the disciples, and that now the teaching would be hers as well, because "Faith comes from hearing."

Once again, Jesus turned the norm on its head and allowed women to break socially defined customs. He liberated Mary from her socially defined status of inferiority and marginalization. Thus, Jesus not only transformed Mary, but the world she inhabited was transformed. Mary became a living translator to influence other women who would never have had the opportunity to hear from a first-hand account.

Mary not only perceives with her own eyes and ears of understanding, but she can change the lives of others through her testimony.

Can't you just imagine the conversation at the local well? And this, I believe, is what Jesus is referring to when He says, "Mary has chosen the better part." Mary not only perceives with her own eyes and ears of understanding, but she can change the lives of others through her testimony.

Back in the kitchen, it seems Martha is perplexed by Mary's behavior. By her own words, she illustrates that she is in the kitchen deciding that simple preparation is not good enough. Only the very best effort will do.

Oh, how I can relate! If my pastor were to come for dinner, I certainly wouldn't serve tuna on toast. "Don't they understand that it takes work and a great deal of effort to get this house in order? Meals just don't appear out of nowhere. Someone has to clean up the mess!"

Distractions begin in our minds. Pots and pans have voices. Don't you realize who is here or who may be dropping by?

Martha begins to prepare a meal that is far beyond what is necessary. She hears the voices called "distractions."

Distractions have other names: guilt and worry. Martha might have asked in her head, "What is Mary doing sitting with the men? This is socially unacceptable. I should go speak to Jesus right now and give Him a piece of my mind. Mary has left me in the kitchen with both of our work. All of this is unacceptable, and I can already see my friends' disapproving eyes."

Martha must have been absolutely fuming, because she doesn't go to Mary and ask her herself; she goes to Jesus to elicit His voice. Can you imagine anyone inter-rupting Jesus? Martha does! I might even go so far as to say that Martha may not even understand why she is so fumed. The very fact that Mary is with "the boys" may have caused her great anxiety, and that is why she goes to Jesus.

Jesus turns to Martha and says, "Martha, Martha, you are so worried and trou-bled [I would add distracted] about so many things."

Of course, Jesus knew what was upsetting Martha. Hers is the voice that resists change.

When my clients get the most stuck about adopting new procedures, it's because they just don't understand how to incorporate these new systems into their lives. Many times, we reject outright something new because change is very difficult, and change—at any level—causes us anxiety. Martha is having to deal with a change in Judaic and social law, and trying to figure out why Messiah is doing this. *This* is what is so upset-ting—change! It is natural to resist change until we understand the "why." And even when we understand the why, it takes habit to fully realize the change into our lives.

This well-known story opens the doorway to the heart of the gospels. Jesus desires to come into our homes, such an ordinary act. He desires a relationship of love, which is reflected in what Paul states in Ephesians 3:17–19:

So that Christ may dwell in your hearts through faith. And I pray that you, being rooted and established in love, may have power, together with all the Lord's holy people, to grasp how wide and long and high and deep is the love of Christ, and to know this love that surpasses knowledge—that you may be filled to the measure of all the fullness of God.

It is Mary who opens her heart to receive Jesus's fulfilling love. Mary is desperate to be taught—so desperate that she breaks Jewish law. This fullness, this incredible love, is the part that can never be taken away from her.

After close examination of this story, it's apparent that the simplicity of the gospel can be found in our ordinary lives. Isn't the whole of the gospel about coming into a relationship with God through His Son, Jesus Christ, and to have that relationship unfold in the ordinary and mundane of life?

Jesus said, "I don't call you servants, I call you friends."

Martha sees Jesus as Messiah, and this fills her with such awe and wonder. She responds by going into the kitchen to serve Him. In others words, Martha serves *for* Jesus. Mary, on the other hand, is known and is being known in a relationship with Jesus.

One attitude says, "I will serve *for* Him," and the other attitude says, "I will serve *from* Him. I will know Him and will be known by Him." Mary chooses to simply love God and to let Him love her as a close and intimate friend, and that response to love will not be taken from her.

This story shows a connection between changes in mindset and priorities. As we change, so will our priorities. What was important yesterday will not be important tomorrow. I have heard it said many times by couples expecting the birth of their firstborn that their thoughts about life have dramatically changed. What they thought about last year is radically different now.

Your Organizing Priorities Today May Change in the Future

Am I advocating that having a well-organized life is not necessary? Of course not!

Where my clients have gone astray is by letting organization alone become the goal, not the process toward their goal. Having the Martha home with "a place for everything and everything in its place" is not the realistic, "life happens," day-to-day atmosphere where most of us live. Leading a well-organized life will let you have the messes and rejoice that at the end of the mess, life will get back together again. There will be no more frustration of not being able to find what you need and no more financial burden of having to buy what you already have, just because you can't find it. Too often our priorities are misguided. Perfection always comes at a cost. What is truly important—relationships—must always come first. Always!

How does this relate to the keeping of our homes when life comes at us with way too much? Whether we are in the office, on the job, in school, or on our knees scrubbing the toilet, understand that all you do is to be done for the glory of God. (1 Corinthians 10:31). This simple story's profound message reminds us that we were created for a purpose; that you are loved by God, and your highest calling is to revel in and respond to His love. That response can come only as you respond to God as an intimate friend. Mary chooses the better, and it will "never be taken from her."

Questions for Reflection:

1. Looking back over your previous week, which of your actions were like Mary?

_____

_____

2. Which were like Martha?

_____

_____

Learning how to separate the important information from the irrelevant sounds simple, but in truth, it is a skill that takes time and consistency to master. Jesus's admonition to Martha that Mary had chosen the "better part" was not only challenging her with a change of new thinking, but also reminding her of the importance of balance and of establishing the proper priorities in her life.

How can we learn to separate the important information from the irrelevant? After all, Jesus's instructions elsewhere in the gospels are to "seek first His kingdom and His righteousness, and all these things will be given to you as well" (Matthew 6:33). As Dallas Willard points out:

"People who are ignorant of God . . . live to eat and drink and dress. For such things the 'gentiles' seek," and their lives are filled with corresponding anxiety and anger and depression about how they will look and how they will fare. By contrast, those who understand Jesus and His Father know that provision has been made for them. Their confidence has been confirmed by their experience. Though they work, they do not worry about things "on earth." Instead, they are always "seeking first the kingdom." That is, they "place top priority on identifying and involving themselves in what God is doing."[16]

Scripture Study

Look up the following verses and write down what God says.

Matthew 6:33

_____

_____

Psalm 42:1

_____

_____

Galatians 1:10

_____

_____

Psalm 105:3–4

_____

_____

Proverbs 8:17

_____

_____

Isaiah 26:3

_____

_____

Organizing Tip: Identifying Your Priorities

When seeking the Lord becomes your priority, all other things will be added unto you. But just like learning a new skill, it takes wisdom and consistency to build the priority muscle.

The good news is that identifying your priorities is a skill you *can* learn. It involves dismissing the less important (for the moment) and narrowing your focus to what is the most critical. Planning your goals and/or days based on your priorities rather than urgency will give you a greater sense of peace and purpose.

Resistance to plans often comes with the mindset that disruptions happen, so why plan? Planning the day will give you a framework from which to work, rather than winging it. The following story from Stephen Covey illustrates this point.

Big Rocks

One day, an expert in time management was speaking to a group of business students. To drive home a point, he used an illustration those students will never forget.

As he stood in front of the group of high-powered overachievers, he said, "Okay, time for a quiz."

He pulled out a one-gallon, wide-mouth Mason jar and set it on the table in front of him. He also produced about a dozen fist-sized rocks and carefully placed them, one at a time, into the jar.

When the jar was filled to the top and no more rocks would fit inside, he asked, "Is this jar full?"

Everyone in the class yelled, "Yes."

The time-management expert replied, "Really?"

He reached under the table and pulled out a bucket of gravel. He dumped some gravel in and shook the jar, causing pieces of gravel to work themselves down into the spaces between the big rocks.

He then asked the group once more, "Is the jar full?"

By this time the class was onto him.

"Probably not," one of them answered.

"Good!" he replied.

He reached under the table and brought out a bucket of sand. He started dumping the sand into the jar, and it went into all of the spaces left between the rocks and the gravel.

Once more he asked the question, "Is this jar full?"

"No!" the class shouted.

Once again, he said, "Good."

Then he grabbed a pitcher of water and began to pour it in until the jar was filled to the brim. Then he looked at the class and asked, "What is the point of this illustration?"

One eager beaver raised his hand and said, "The point is, no matter how full your schedule, if you try really hard you can always fit some more things in it!"

"No," the speaker replied. "That's not the point. The truth this illustration teaches us is: If you don't put the big rocks in first, you'll never get them in at all!"[17]

What are the "big rocks" in your life? Is it time with your loved ones, your faith, your education, your dreams, a worthy cause, or teaching or mentoring others? Remember to put these *big rocks* in your jar first, or you'll never get them in at all.

To Think About

Here are a few example questions regarding daily priorities.

- Should I sort through emails or continue writing?
- Should I cook dinner or exercise?
- Should I take a friend to lunch or go to the church prayer meeting?
- Should I plan my menu for the week or go for a walk with my son?

List the top three priorities in your life now.

1. _____
2. _____
3. _____

This decision-making process is often guided by the following questions:

1. What is your most urgent and important need? Is there anything that is time sensitive?

_____

_____

2. How much energy will it take, either physically or mentally?

_____

_____

3. Should you do it first thing in the morning or wait until later?

_____

_____

4. Is there anyone that you need to help you make this decision?

_____

_____

5. Is there anyone you can delegate this task to?

_____

_____

If you don't plan your week, your week will plan itself. When you allow your calendar to fill up with things that don't reflect your values and priorities, you'll find yourself frustrated by the end of the week.

Finally, when you begin your day in God's presence, you'll have clearer and more purposeful thinking. Take time to rest in the Lord's presence.

Organizing Tip: Understanding the Roles You Play

Developing deeper relationships takes time and commitment. Here are a few ways to keep your time organized as you nurture existing relationships and develop new ones.

Define your key roles. Are you a:

- Mother/father?
- Wife/husband?
- Sister/brother?
- Friend?
- Volunteer?
- Business owner or employee?
- Dancer or singer?
- Scout leader or sports coach?
- Yourself as an individual

This list is only an example of some of the roles/hats many of us wear each day.

Most of my clients fall into the life-_reactive_ trap instead of having a _pro_active lifestyle. For example, one of my clients had on her role list that she was an aunt—it was a priority for her. Her nephew was on the baseball league at school, and she made a verbal commitment to attend one of his home games. Sadly, the season came and went, and she totally forgot to add his schedule to her planner. In fact, she never used a planner. As a result, her nephew was very disappointed that she never showed up to any of his games. So how do you avoid these kinds of oversights?

Begin using either a paper or electronic planner, listing all the roles in your life.

Take your month-at-a-glance, and schedule in time for each of the roles/relationships that are important to you. If we never take the time to develop our relationships, sooner or later they will suffer.

Take thirty to sixty minutes per week to schedule your roles/priorities.

Remember only *you* can take care of *you*. Only *you* can keep *you* healthy. Only *you* can be responsible for *your* choices.

Rosa's Story

One of my personal frustrations, and a reason why organization took so long to become a priority in my life, was that getting organized took time away from my ministry. I began to realize that God brings order wherever He goes, and that the people I minister to are calmer and more open when the room in which I welcome them is calmer and more ordered. I am also more focused on them when I am not thinking, *I hope they don't see the wrappers on the floor!* Now I see that getting organized internally and externally is an important part of serving God with all my other gifts. It facilitates my effectiveness. I try hard to keep it in the job description.

At first, Martha did not understand Jesus's invitation to have Mary listen to His teachings. It is my hope that it didn't take Martha long to change her priorities. Our new priorities are the end result of understanding new concepts, and require changes of both mind and behavior. Changing the way we think will produce the activities and desires that God has planned for our day.

Questions for Reflection:

1. Was there a time this past week when "life happened," and you couldn't get it all done?

_____

_____

2. In what ways can you relate to Karen's story at the beginning of this chapter?

_____

_____

3. How do disorganization or poor time management hinder you in your "purpose for the day"?

_____

_____

4. What are the "big rocks" in your life?

_____

_____

Redeeming Your Time

No matter where I go—working side-by-side with a client, working virtually across the globe, or speaking to hundreds of people in churches—I'm always asked one question:

"How do I get more hours in my day?"

There is so much going on in the world these days that our schedules quickly fill. Related to priorities, we need to constantly work toward maintaining the balance between self, family, and outside demands.

One of the teachers for *Get Organized God's Way* suggested that we tell our students to create what she termed "margins" in our schedules. Similar to the margins in a book, our time margins help us to create extra space and to use time effectively. I liken it to the drawers in our home. If we continue to cram too much stuff into our drawers, eventually we can't see what's in there, and everything is either ignored or misplaced. Time is the same way. By cramming too much into our schedules, we lose sight of what is truly important and lose our ability to prioritize meaning in the day.

Examples of adding margin are:

- Arriving early to appointments so you can give full attention to the meeting instead of rushing from one place to the other.
- Planning the day ahead. I find that when clients plan their day the night before, they no longer lose sleep regarding missed activities or tomorrow's schedule. Waking up refreshed can make every relationship and task more positive.

When we realize God has given our time—like our treasures—to us, we will value it more and focus on the right priorities. In creating this balance, we will be more energized, and our days will be more rewarding. Giving our best each day will create an authentic walk with the Lord.

Taking It to God

Father,

I want to dedicate every aspect of my life to Jesus so I can operate in the Holy Spirit's power and strength. I am insufficient to meet the needs of my home and the priorities necessary to keep it running. At times, it just seems so overwhelming, but I can do all things through Christ Jesus who strengthens me. This doesn't mean I can continue to pile more activities and demands into my schedule. Instead, help me to first learn the art of prioritizing and then have the strength to carry out those priorities. Help me, dear God, to know when to say yes and when to say no. Keep my life in perfect balance so I can experience perfect peace. Above all, it's my relationships that matter most, not my activities or possessions. Thank You for the hope based on those decisions and choices I make today. I praise You, God, who blesses me with wisdom and peace. Amen.

Chapter 5
A Simple Life Brings Abundance

He must increase, but I must decrease.
John 3:30 KJV

With today's breakneck pace of instant information, multitasking mania, and task tyranny, ask anyone how they are doing. If they are being honest, somewhere in the conversation they'll tell you that they are overwhelmed. Sunday sermons are filled with the urgency to put God first, and Christians may be convicted to change. This fast-paced lifestyle is not what God intended for us, yet the idea of simplifying our lives seems like a distant dream. In John 3:30 (the above scripture), John is speaking literally about *his* ministry, but Christians can borrow the same mindset and apply it to their own lives.

The following definition of "organizing" reflects this intended mindset:

Organization is not what you see on TV. It's not about color-coordinated containers and indexed filing systems and someone coming in to do a "clean sweep" on your clutter, just so you can go out and buy more stuff and have somewhere to put it. It's not about quick fixes or control. Organization is about living simply, paying attention to your actions, making conscious choices. Simplifying our lives, restoring balance and meaning, feeling connected to a power greater than ourselves—these are the core of being organized. This sense of connection and meaning is what we hunger for—and mistakenly try to fill with things.[18]

The definitions of *organization* and *organic* have the same root meaning: whole, complete, and one. When we feel complete and whole, we no longer need to fill the empty void with more and more material goods. Organizing illuminates the effect our possessions have on our life. Organization is not about simply cleaning up; it's about making mindful decisions about life.

> *Organization is not about simply cleaning up; it's about making mindful decisions about life.*

In the organizing process, one begins to understand that simplicity is a hallmark to an orderly life. Pam and Chuck D. Pierce say in *The Rewards of Simplicity*, "The purpose of simplicity is not to prune away those things that bring us joy and enrich our lives. Instead, the purpose of simplicity is to streamline our lives in such a way that we have more room, time, and energy for the pursuits and people that God ordains for us."[19]

What Is Simple Living?

Simple living is not a fad; it's a way of life. It's about getting creative, being content, and learning how to do more with less. We are bombarded daily with advertisements and sales that try to convince us that true happiness comes from having more, especially more than everybody else. Our society measures the health of our economy by how much we spend and generally believes that more is better. Yet it's

> *Clutter steals all life from a room and those who occupy it. Clutter robs us of peace of mind.*

important to understand that *it's not the amount of stuff* but *the quality of the stuff and how it relates to our lives* that *really matters*. Clutter steals all life from a room and those who occupy it.

Clutter robs us of peace of mind. When we are constantly thinking about what to do with our stuff, it keeps us from thinking thoughts that can bring us joy.

Simple living, also called "voluntary simplicity," is making the decision *not* to accumulate more stuff here on earth but to live your life storing up heavenly treasures.

> Store up for yourselves treasures in heaven, where moths and vermin do not destroy, and where thieves do not break in and steal. (Matthew 6:20b)

Sheila's Story

John the Baptist knew that he was called to prepare the way of the Lord. He was to point others to the One who could save them. He knew this power to save others was not his. He simply directed people to Jesus.

A Christian life is a life transformed, but somehow, I'm in a holding pattern. I keep doing the same things and thinking the same thoughts and expecting different outcomes. How can I become more effective for His kingdom when others cannot see a difference in my life because of Him? In fact, the enemy tells me that my unsaved loved ones lead a more virtuous life than I do and therefore are less in need of salvation.

I keep asking myself why I should accrue more and more goods beyond need, to the point of wasteful clutter. My house isn't hospitable. I am stymied from reaching out to others with graciousness to woo them to Christ. How can I witness His love when my door remains closed? How can I maintain relationships while keeping family and friends at a distance, never letting them fully know the station of my life, never granting them the intimacy so necessary for closeness? I must decrease my junk that He might shine out in the spaciousness of a home dedicated to His glory.

I have decided not to hide under a bushel. I will show others my problem, and at the same time, I will trust God to grow me into the mature, God-reflecting woman I'm called to be. I pray that in showing others the process of my struggle into victory, God will be glorified and I will be de-emphasized. The power to conquer this problem lies not in me but in my Savior. Lord, help me submit to Your perfect will so that You will be gloriously showcased in my home, my family, and my life.

Questions for Reflection:

1. Was there a time this past week when you felt overwhelmed with stuff?

_____

_____

2. Where can you apply voluntary simplicity in your daily life?

_____

_____

Scripture Study

Look up the following verses and write down what God says.

Matthew 19:24 and 1 Corinthians 13:3
How do these verses relate to simplifying your life?

_____

_____

Matthew 18:2–3 and 2 Corinthians 1:12
What does it mean to have simplicity of heart?

_____

_____

Galatians 5:16
How does walking in the Spirit coincide with simplifying your life?

_____

_____

Author and professional organizer Peter Walsh states, "It's impossible to make your best decisions, your most enlightened, spiritually rich, emotionally stable choices, in a cluttered and disorganized home. It just can't happen. Time and time again, I have seen that when you open the space, you create the opportunity for amazing things to flow into that space."[20]

John 3:30 tells us to decrease and let God increase, and that will set your gaze and feet onto the path toward organization and simplicity.

Simple Living Is Just Plain Hard!

The following quote is from *Freedom of Simplicity* by Richard J. Foster:

But please, do not misinterpret simplicity with "simplism." Whether we peer into the universe of the telescope or the universe of the microscope, we cannot help being amazed at the varied complexity of the created order. From galaxy to ant to atom, we are awed by the intricate mosaic. . . . As the psalmist declared, we are indeed "fearfully and wonderfully made."[21]

Life is full of paradoxes, and simple living is not easily mastered. The Bible paints the same picture in Matthew 10:39 and Luke 6:38 (to gain life we must lose it, and in giving we receive).

Without the combined efforts of community, achieving a simpler lifestyle on one's own is especially hard. It is like swimming upstream without the support of others to maintain your decisions. Simplicity involves a consciously chosen course of actions involving both individual and group life. Getting your family and church on board is a great first step in your lifestyle transformation.

> The primary reason people don't receive the light that would open them up to a better understanding of God is that life is simply too complex.
> —Mac Hammond[22]

To Think About

He must increase . . .

In our struggle to loosen ourselves from the entangling net of clutter, we may lose sight of an important factor: it's not about us. Above all, Jesus demands that we love Him more than anyone or anything—that we follow Him, trust Him, enjoy Him, be satisfied in Him, delight in Him, and obey Him. The world screams to do this or buy that. When Jesus becomes greater in my world, and I become lesser in my world, my joy increases. "He must increase, but I must decrease" (John 3:30 KJV). This lesson has taken me many, many years to learn, and it is one that I must keep focused on every day.

We must decrease . . .

Rachael's Story

I overdo. I apply this approach to many things. I overdo on clothing. I want things to be perfect for every occasion, so I must have a great variety in order to have just the right outfit. I overdo on planning and tend to put too many jobs on my schedule. I overdo in my research or information gathering to find just the right set of dishes or the right car to buy. I overdo on my hobbies by buying more materials than I need. I am now beginning to understand that my overdoing is due to the need to be perfect, and my perfectionism leads me to excess. I now understand that less is truly more and that I can accomplish more when I am truly present and focused on a task. No longer do the "what ifs" reside in my brain. Letting go or decreasing actually allows me to increase the joy and love in my life.

When our hearts are satisfied, we don't need to keep so much or do so much. If we feel at peace internally, we don't feel the need to hang on to so much stuff that it turns into clutter and junk. When we have a sense that life is positive, we'll find it easier to let go of many things (time commitments and physical objects) without a sense of personal loss. Identifying our priorities in life and letting go of the things that do not enhance those priorities is the key to an orderly life.

At the heart of organization is a lifestyle of "just enough." However, to obtain a balance, you must continually readdress the definition of "just enough." The truest way to obtain that just enough balance is through prayer. Simplicity and prayer are woven together through trust—trusting that God will hear and will bring about the outcome according to His perfect will. Without trust, we might grab hold of the idea that we need to keep stuff "just in case." Our materialistic training to acquire keeps us in a constant battle with our spirit's desire to live free from this burden.

Our material blessings are not for us alone, but for the good of all. God's great generosity allows us to model that generosity to others. Because He gave, we are enabled to give. Simple living means that we trust God for His provisions and that what we have comes from His generous hand. Trusting frees us to give from a grateful heart, knowing that we give because we were given to.

The writer of Hebrews encourages us:

Simple living means that we trust God for His provisions and that what we have comes from His generous hand.

Keep your lives free from the love of money and be content with what you have, because God has said, "Never will I leave you; never will I forsake you." So we say with confidence, "The Lord is my helper; I will not be afraid. What can mere mortals do to me?" (Hebrews 13:5–6)

There are two ways to get enough. One is to continue to accumulate more and more. The other is to desire less. —G. K. Chesterton[23]

How to Decrease

What is your definition of "just enough?"

_____

_____

By decreasing your stuff, time, and activities, do you see your life increasing in meaningful ways?

_____

_____

If so, how?

_____

_____

Give an example of "less is more."

_____

_____

What does it mean to you that, "He must increase, but I must decrease"?

_____

_____

Go confidently in the directions of your dreams; live the life you've imagined. As you simplify your life, the laws of the universe will be simpler. —Henry David Thoreau[24]

Organizing Tip: Living Abundantly

More stuff doesn't equate with an abundant life. On the contrary, a lot of stuff drains your life and relationships. The demon called "scarcity" is the belief that there is not enough to go around: not enough money, jobs, energy, or love. It's a fear that you may be left out. Panic sets in and you grab for things that bring you comfort and security.

Abundance is the belief that what you have at this very moment is all you need. Transforming your mindset from one of scarcity to one of trust will free you from anxieties, worries, and futile ambitions, replacing them with blessings.

Here are a few tips to make abundance flow into your life:

- Look around your living space and decide what you haven't touched in a year or longer. Which items might be useful to someone else? Gather up what you no longer use and donate it.
- Examine the motivation behind your buying habits. Do you buy for approval? Is it a need or just a want?
- Pay attention when the stock-up-for-just-in-case instinct kicks in. Buying in bulk is not the bargain you think it is. Do you find comfort in surplus? Do you fear you really will never have enough?

COVID had a profound impact on our thinking regarding our stock-up mindset. I remember clearly the shelves of toilet paper and paper towels being empty and wondering just why these particular objects were at the forefront of this scarcity mentality.

Moving toward a simpler lifestyle is not the same for everyone. Some people might want to simplify their buying habits, examining their motivations behind each purchase. Others may want to just deal with less in their lives. Less stuff equals less stress. Ask yourself these questions:

- Does this add meaning/value to my life?
- If this was in a store, would I want to buy it?
- How important is this to me?
- Does this conflict with or enhance my priorities?
- Could I eliminate this from my life?

Remember, simplicity is not easy. Doing the simple thing by faith is much more difficult than maintaining the status quo in our overly complex world. Old habits die hard, and it takes discipline and practice. Begin by surrounding yourself with a community of those that will encourage and motivate you along this journey.

Economist and statistician E. F. Schumacher said, "Any intelligent fool can make things bigger, more complex, and more violent. It takes a touch of genius—and a lot of courage—to move in the opposite direction."[25]

Taking It to God

Lord Jesus,

When I look around at all the material blessings You have poured into my life, I am overwhelmed. Overwhelmed that You have given me my heart's desire, but also overwhelmed that I did not put limits on these material wants, for they are now overtaking my home. Thank You for shining Your light inside me and exposing these areas of excess.

Your Word teaches that Your yoke is easy. However, my life is anything but easy. I have overscheduled my time; I have overbought my wardrobe; I have overdone my to-dos. I now run to Your throne room and ask You to teach me the valuable steps to simplifying my life. I now understand that less is more and that You alone are sufficient.

I also now know that simple living is the only way that I can truly know Your plan for my life. Deuteronomy 30:11–14 reminds me, "Now what I am commanding you today is not too difficult for you or beyond your reach. It is not up in heaven, so that you have to ask, 'Who will ascend into heaven to get it and proclaim it to us so we may obey it?' Nor is it beyond the sea, so that you have to ask, 'Who will cross the sea to get it and proclaim it to us so we may obey it?' No, the Word is very near you; it is in your mouth and in your heart so you may obey it."

Your Word is a reminder that this is not too difficult for me and that living simply is not beyond my reach. Help me to know Your Word and to daily profess it with my mouth so that my heart may obey it. Teach me, dear Lord. Amen.

Chapter 6
Giving God's Way or the World's Way: Give and It Will Be Given to You

One person gives freely, yet gains even more; another withholds unduly, but comes to poverty.

Proverbs 11:24

Give freely and become more wealthy; be stingy and lose everything.

Proverbs 11:24 NLT

Is there a connection between generosity and wealth as Proverbs 11:24 states? If God's Word is truth, then what is the connection between ownership and poverty? What is the difference between living with a spirit of "open hands" and living with a spirit of "grasping and clinging?" The world rationalizes that the more we give away, the less we will have; conversely, the more we hang onto, the more we will have. What if Proverbs 11:24 is true? The verse seems to be saying the exact opposite of what the world tells us.

> It is possible to give away and become richer, it is also possible to hold on too tightly and lose everything. Generous people shall be rich—by watering others they water themselves. —Timothy R. Botts, *The Biblical Year*

Proverbs 11:25 says, "A generous person will prosper; whoever refreshes others will be refreshed." The original Hebrew for generous is blessing, and the word translated man [or person] is really soul. Therefore, "a soul of blessing" will prosper. Also, the word refreshes is taken from "to water". If we choose to let water flow from us, out of a soul that desires to bless, then the refreshing water flows to us as well. Jesus said that the one who believes in him, streams of living water will flow from within them.[26]

I'm sure you're thinking, *How very spiritual. So what does this have to do with organizing?*

In my organizing assessment session with my clients, I explain that the process of organizing must begin with an examination of the excess, of what is causing the dysfunction of the room. Creating a vision for the area and making a criteria list of what will stay and what will go is essential for any success. As Wesley Zinn elaborates, if your stream of water (representing your mind and space) is dammed up, "the water begins to stagnate and become unhealthy."

Some examples of things that could dam up our minds like a rock would be either not trusting God to provide for our daily needs or holding on to our possessions in hopes that they might be needed someday. Living with a new mindset of giving instead of keeping for a just-in-case day results in a new flow of generosity of heart.

> Fresh blessing and refreshing water continues to flow [once this is realized] . . . A soul that desires to bless is what opens the flow, and the purpose of the flow is to continue to bless. A spirit of poverty clings to what one has and is afraid of losing it. The problem is that the very act of clinging stops up the flow. The word for poverty in Hebrew is derived from the word lack. Therefore, the spirit of poverty inflicts poverty.[27]

To Think About

What do you think this means: "Out of a spirit of generosity flows a wellspring of life"?

_____

_____

How does this translate into a different organizing mindset?

_____

_____

> Give, and it will be given to you. Good measure, pressed down, shaken together, running over, will be put into your lap. For with the measure you use it will be measured back to you. (Luke 6:38)

Kale's Story

I was one of ten people helping to clear out my newly deceased aunt and uncle's home. Their hobby over the years of their retirement was getting stuff for free with coupons. They had saved everything they ever owned. It was so hard to sort through it all.

We filled one dumpster with stuff and another dumpster was coming. I had made several trips to the donation drop-off place. When I returned and looked around, it seemed as if we had hardly begun. This was the most stressful job I had ever undertaken, even with so many people helping. Looking at the food pantry, we found free canned goods they had acquired with coupons. So much waste!

In contrast, this reminded me of a testimony someone had once told me. An aunt had lived a long and wonderful life. The church was packed for her funeral. Choir members were barely able to sing at her funeral because so many in the choir were crying or trying to hold back the tears. Even the minister was visibly saddened at the loss of this dear sister. Many people stood to speak, remembering the kindnesses that this woman had shown them over the years. She would truly be missed by people of all ages. She had lived with her sister, and all she left behind were the items that she loved the most. Incredibly, they all could fit in the trunk of a car with room to spare.

The experience of clearing out my aunt and uncle's home taught me that things acquired for free come with a high price. If they are hoarded and not passed on to those who can use them, they can truly burden us physically and emotionally. I am grateful to be able to see the difference between a woman who traveled light, yet left much goodness behind, and my relatives. What the hoarders left was much stress for their heirs.

In preparation for dying, it occurs to me that I would not want to leave a bunch of junk behind for my kids to have to sort through and dispose of. I want to travel light and spend my time and energy helping people and just loving them.

Remember this:

Whoever sows sparingly will also reap sparingly, and whoever sows generously will also reap generously. (2 Corinthians 9:6)

In the kingdom of God, the physical laws are much different from those of earth. When we believe, all things are possible. God's giving principle is illustrated by the following story in Matthew 14.

God Is an Abundant Giver

The book of Matthew tells us:

> Prompted by her mother, she [Salome] said, "Give me here on a platter the head of John the Baptist." The king was distressed, but because of his oaths and his dinner guests, he ordered that her request be granted and had John beheaded in the prison. His head was brought in on a platter and given to the girl, who carried it to her mother. John's disciples came and took his body and buried it. Then they went and told Jesus.
>
> When Jesus heard what had happened, he withdrew by boat privately to a solitary place. Hearing of this, the crowds followed him on foot from the towns. When Jesus landed and saw a large crowd, he had compassion on them and healed their sick. As evening approached, the disciples came to him and said, "This is a remote place, and it's already getting late. Send the crowds away, so they can go to the villages and buy themselves some food." Jesus replied, "They do not need to go away. You give them something to eat." "We have here only five loaves of bread and two fish," they answered. "Bring them here to me," he said. And he directed the people to sit down on the grass. Taking the five loaves and the two fish and looking up to heaven, he gave thanks and broke the loaves. Then he gave them to the disciples, and the disciples gave them to the people. They all ate and were satisfied, and the disciples picked up twelve basketfuls of broken pieces that were left over. The number of those who ate was about five thousand men, besides women and children. (Matthew 14:8–23)

Let's set the stage. Jesus has just learned of John the Baptist's beheading. He withdraws to a solitary and remote place a few miles from Bethesda.

The word "solitary" denotes a space that is desolate, free from distractions. My clients often complain of hundreds of distractions in the day. A cluttered area is one of the most distracting places to be. But notice that it is in this *solitary* place that Jesus withdraws to spend time with the Father.

Then the people see Jesus, and many begin to follow Him. Their individual agendas are tossed aside because hearing Jesus is what now matters most. The crowd is desperate to be taught and to be touched. Jesus has compassion on them and heals their sick. His disciples notice that the demands on Jesus are great. Evening is rapidly approaching. They go to Jesus to tell Him to send the crowd away so they can buy food for themselves. It would seem that the disciples are more concerned about their being fed than about the healings.

Matthew 14:17 states that in the crowd there is a young boy who offers up his meager lunch—all that he has. He gives it to the disciples to feed the crowd.

"Here is a boy with five small barley loaves and two small fish, but how far will they go among so many?" (John 6:9).

When the disciples asked the crowd that day for a bit of food, as instructed by Jesus, they had no idea what was about to unfold. Giving to others must have been second nature to this lad, who offered up all that he had by faith. By giving away his lunch, God used his gift and multiplied it to satisfy thousands.

In Matthew 14:19, Jesus takes the loaves and fish, gives thanks while breaking the bread, and then the disciples distribute *as much as they wanted* to those who are seated.

He says to His disciples in John 6:12, referring to the same event, "Gather the pieces that are left over. Let nothing be wasted."

As an organizer, my heart rejoices over the fact that in the kingdom of God, nothing goes to waste. *Everything* and *everyone* has meaning and purpose.

In Matthew 14:20, the disciples pick up *twelve* basketfuls of leftovers, but then nothing is said about what they do with all those half-eaten loaves. I think that God purposed not to tell us so that we will ponder the meaning of spiritual leftovers. In our mundane daily life, we tend to dispose of that which we feel is irrelevant or insignificant. But God says all is relevant, all is significant, even leftover bread. When we give, God increases our giving. Those that receive your offering are blessed, but more importantly, it is in the giving of those blessings that God moves His plans and purposes in your life. Like those leftovers, we may not see the outcome, but we do know that God is moving mightily for His children!

What is there in your spiritual life that Jesus doesn't want to go to waste? It is in our giving that God distributes to the fullest. Some may hold on to things, thinking wrongly that they do not want to waste what they have received. But by clinging to our stuff, *we* hinder God's purpose to bless others.

God Loves . . . God Gives

> For God so loved the world, that he gave his only begotten Son, that whosoever believeth in him should not perish, but have everlasting life. (John 3:16 KJV)

Pause for a moment at the words . . . loved and gave. God first loved . . . and then he gave.

When I think back to my early days of romantic love, I remember my intense feelings. What better way to act on those wondrous feelings but to give? Not just the stuff that I knew my boyfriend would adore, but the giving of my time and attention.

But that giving was not enough. I also gave my will away. I would not hesitate to do what he wanted or go where he wanted to go. Of course, in a healthy relationship these are reciprocated, but the act remained. I gave up my own desires to please the one I loved. When we love, giving is a natural by-product. God so loved the world that He gave . . .

Jesus so loved the Father that He gave up His will on the cross to do His Father's work. It's easy to give, to be kind and to do good to others who are always being kind, doing good, and blessing others. Jesus said that even the sinners (the world) do those things. As Christians, we are supposed to do the opposite of the world's way. That is why Jesus says to do these things for people who are not kind, and we will benefit from it.

How?

For with the measure you use when you grant or bestow an act of kindness, a charitable deed, or helpfulness to others, it will be measured back to you.

> Give, and it will be given to you. A good measure, pressed down, shaken together and running over, will be poured into your lap. For with the measure you use, it will be measured to you. (Luke 6:38)

Give away to everyone who has a need and do not take back your goods from someone who has taken from you, and your needs will be met, and what has been taken from you will be given back; pressed down, shaken together, and running over.

This truth is illustrated in a story by Joyce Meyer. The story is recalled about a bracelet Joyce owned. One day, Joyce was prompted to give the bracelet away. After much grumbling and arguing with all the reasons she should keep the bracelet, God won out, and she gave it away.

However, her heart was not in the giving. After many months, she saw the woman who had received the bracelet, and she returned the bracelet to Joyce. However, Joyce never seemed to enjoy wearing it again, for it had lost its luster and desire even though it looked exactly the same. The blessing of the bracelet was lost. Joyce says she keeps the item to remind herself to give with a generous heart so that she will bless others as God continues to bless her.

Giving with a compassionate heart freely opens up the heavens for you to receive God's riches and best.[28]

Letting Go: The Real Versus the Imitation

God wants to pour out His abundant blessings on those who trust in Him. His provisions are endless, and at the same time, meaningful, satisfying, and eternal. God also wants to give His children His very best. Sadly, we settle time after time for the second rate or an imitation.

Every summer when I was a child, my family would make "real" ice cream in a hand-crank machine. My taste buds had a party every time I licked the paddle. Carton ice cream never really measured up, and I would count the months until, once again, the real stuff would pass my tongue.

It's much the same once we've experienced God's genuine blessings. Nothing less will do.

God wants to pour out His abundant blessings on those who trust in Him. His provisions are endless, and at the same time, meaningful, satisfying, and eternal.

Janine's Story

I have to tell you something pretty amazing that happened to me today.

Several weeks back, I contacted the studio of a renowned artist whose work I particularly admire. I was fortunate to have the artist herself answer the phone, and we visited for a few minutes. I asked her about a couple of small items from her collection that I wanted to purchase for my children.

In the course of talking with her, I commented on how I had always admired a large print of a certain work of hers, but probably would not be able to afford it for some time due to circumstances in my life. During our conversation, it became apparent that she also had a deep faith in God. She encouraged me and said she would pray for me. She told me that when I sent the payment for the items I was ordering, to attach a note indicating I had talked with her.

Earlier this week while I was straightening up, I came across the brochure from her studio with a photo of the long-desired art print in it. I thought, *I won't be able to order this for a very long time, so in the meantime it's taking up precious space in my home.* With a sad resolve, I put it in the recycling bin.

Today, the mailman knocked at my door with a large package. The artist had sent me a signed and numbered artist's proof, which is even more valuable than the signed limited edition print I had been wanting!

Enclosed with the package was a hand-written note of encouragement. The note closed with, "This one's on me—enjoy!"

Isn't God good? I thought of the spiritual parallel in this story. God wants us to get rid of the imitation, the pale facsimile of His best for us, so that He can give us His real best for us—the genuine article—rather than just what looks similar to it. In light of His desire to give us His best, how can we continue to fail to seek after it and do our part? It's this very thought which spurs me on through the difficult process of reordering my home to conform more closely to the image of the orderly God in whose likeness I was created.

For if we are all created in His likeness, and He has set each star and planet in its place, then this is how He orders His universe, His home. I need to do the same for my home as well.

Scripture Study

Look up the following verses. What is the spiritual principle in giving?

Proverbs 3:9

_____

_____

2 Corinthians 9:6

_____

_____

2 Corinthians 9:7

_____

_____

Deuteronomy 16:17

_____

_____

Acts 20:35

_____

_____

1 Timothy 6:6–7, 17–19

_____

_____

Organizing Tip: The A-Time-to-Keep-and-a-Time-to-Throw-Away Principle

Have you heard of the *Pareto Principle,* also known as the 80/20 rule? Allow me to share a little bit about this rule and how it relates to organizing.

There was an Italian scientist named Vilfredo Pareto, who discovered through observation that 80 percent of Italian land was owned by only 20 percent of the population. He also observed that 20 percent of his peapods contained 80 percent of the peas in his garden. He, along with other scientists and thinkers, started to apply this idea to other areas of study—like mathematics and science. They soon discovered that this idea of "roughly 80 percent of the effects come from 20 percent of the causes" was actually common.

The Pareto Principle also applies to a variety of other items and events:

- We wear only 20 percent of our clothing 80 percent of the time.
- We spend 80 percent of our time with 20 percent of our acquaintances.
- 80 percent of our interruptions come from the same 20 percent of people.
- 20 percent of the work we do consumes 80 percent of our time and resources.
- We reference/retrieve 20 percent of our paper files 80 percent of the time.

You can apply the 80/20 rule to almost anything, from business operations and time-management principles to clutter and physical possessions. The exact percentages may vary, but the overall gist of the principle remains the same.

So, turning that around, basically 80 percent of your items are only being used 20 percent of the time. And I would venture to guess that there are items, clothing, and paper files that will never be seen or used again! Can you imagine how much more space you'd have if you condensed your possessions down to just those that are your favorites and that you actually use? Wow! We'd all be living in homes half the size!

> *Can you imagine how much more space you'd have if you condensed your possessions down to just those that are your favorites and that you actually use?*

Is it realistic for you to downsize that drastically? Probably not. But if you are faced with space issues in your closet, kitchen, or office, consider Pareto and his principle; it just might help you let go of 80 percent of the stuff you rarely use.

Once you can accept and internalize this principle, it can create lasting change in your buying habits. Remember, this is a guideline for sharpening your perception of how you use your possessions.

According to the Pareto Principle, a person might have the following at home:

- Thirty pairs of shoes, six of them worn regularly
- Five pairs of jeans, but one favorite
- Ten lipsticks and two used daily
- Two hundred CDs, 160 of which have been played once

So how does the Pareto Principle relate to giving? Once you understand that you really need only 20 percent in a certain category, your ability to release the 80 percent will become a reality in your life. How many ice cream scoops do you really need? Blessing others with what is excess in your home is one way of honoring what God gave you.

It has been said that God wants to make us happy. In doing so, He blesses us with material goods. Once these goods have served their purpose and we only hang on to them out of fear, God will no longer bless us with the enjoyment of having them.

When we center our thoughts on who can make use of our excess in a positive way, letting go seems easier. We know they will be given new life and be appreciated. Giving to a women's shelter, to those escaping a violent life, or to someone affected by the loss of a home through fire or forces of nature are only a few suggestions for whom we might give our excess to.

Tracy's Story

The Pareto Principle was a revelation. Knowing that I use approximately 20 percent of my things has me looking at my home in a new way. I've been imagining what living with only the 20 percent would look like. In every drawer, every closet, and every cabinet—what if I eliminated 80 percent of its contents and kept 20 percent? Or if I just reduce it down 50 percent? Or what if I just went through every hiding spot/drawer/cabinet/storage container and threw away everything that I didn't need?

It is amazing how strong a hold my "stuff" has on me. So many memories keep me from getting rid of books and papers. It is really hard to let go. I can't imagine what it would be like not to have those ties, and I must admit that I am scared not to have them.

But after reading this chapter, I've been imagining how God would fill that void. What will happen if I got rid of those college books that I hardly remember and will probably never reread? Or what about those old work files that I keep in case I ever need to go back to work? Or those old toys that I think my kids will miss, but they haven't seen since I packed them in boxes a few years ago? I am starting to see how free I would feel if I didn't have so many old things and I had space for the "new."

My new interests and new hobbies have no place in my home. All of the new stuff has become a large pile next to my computer, and I usually throw those things away first. What if I got rid of the old to make room for the new? My mind is still wrapping around this. Making room for God's blessings always seems to be something spiritual. I never saw it as physical. The connection between the two now seems so obvious. I can't believe I've never thought about it until now.

Being organized does not come easily, but like any skill, I'm working on it and letting God guide my steps. I'm becoming more disciplined and more confident as I tackle my home. Even my kids are becoming more organized. I am less stressed, and I have time to celebrate when I get one step closer to my goal of an organized life. Truly, this is changing everything.

Taking It to God

Father,

You are the supplier of all. I have forgotten that all things come from You. I have held to my materialistic mindset out of fear—fear that I will need that thing one day or that I will never be able to afford another. Lord, I need You to stand with me today and help me to further Your purposes by ridding myself of unneeded things—by passing along what I can to someone who will use it, and by throwing out what is truly junk. Give me the wisdom to know the difference. Forgive me for the stuff I have bought, spending money recklessly and junking up my house with stuff that will never bring me joy. I ask You to help me forgive myself so that I can stop feeling guilty for it all. Enable me to walk closer to You while I clean up all the excess.

In the name of Jesus, I bind this consuming spirit and cast it into the abyss. Help me understand that there is a season to keep and a season to discard. As my life continues on its journey, help me to see the truth of a future that has promise and beautiful spaces to fill. Help me to develop a generous heart. Help me discern what is of true value and what is imitation. I have been swept up in the lie that says if it's a bargain, I can't pass it up. I trust You to transform my beliefs and transform who I am. You are the King of the universe—all things are Yours. I am heir to that crown and that makes me a prince or princess. I believe You will pour out Your blessings upon me as I let go and receive my fullest potential. I understand now what a true blessing is—reaching my fullest potential. Amen.

Chapter 7
An Idol Called Clutter: The Power of Stuff

You know that when you were pagans, somehow or other you were influenced and led astray to mute idols.

1 Corinthians 12:2

Remember how you were when you didn't know God, led from one phony god to another, never knowing what you were doing, just doing it because everybody else did it? It's different in this life. God wants us to use our intelligence, to seek to understand as well as we can.

1 Corinthians 12:2 MSG

In my BC days (before Christ), I used to pay a great amount of attention to stuff! Home furnishings, fashion, seeking out the "right" friends, and putting on a great display of what I thought a close and wonderful family life should look like. It was exhausting, to say the least. My own desires became the focus of my days, and I was terribly unsatisfied with the path my life was taking. Possessions, the right job, the right friends, and even family became the center of my world. I would have never thought that these desires were *idols*, but in hindsight, that was exactly what they were.

Then Jesus entered my life, and *everything* changed. All of these desires lost their stronghold, and seeking Him became the focus of my attention. No longer was I exhausted in my daily life, but joy and purpose began to reign.

In the twenty-first century, no one would say I created idols in my life, but God makes it very clear, when we desire anything else more than we do Him, it is an idol.

Idols have a way of leading us astray. They set us up for a life of strife and unfulfilled expectations based on how we think our lives should look.

Idols have a way of leading us astray. They set us up for a life of strife and unfulfilled expectations based on how we think our lives should look.

The Lust for Idols: A Matter of the Heart

What is idolatry? Simply stated, an idol is anything or anyone we hold above God.

We think that idols are bad things, but that is almost never the case. The greater the good, the more likely we are to expect that it can satisfy our deepest needs and hopes. Anything can serve as a counterfeit god, especially the very best things in life. —Timothy Keller, *Counterfeit Gods*[29]

The evil in our desire typically does not lie in what we want, but that we want it too much. —John Calvin

What Is Your Idol?

- Wealth can be an idol.
- Popularity can be an idol.
- Possessions can be an idol.
- Career can be an idol.
- Family can be an idol.

These things in and of themselves are not inherently evil. Ezekiel 14:3 (NASB) says:

Son of man, these men have set up their idols in their hearts, and have put right before their faces the stumbling block of their iniquity.

It is in the *wanting* of those things where we get into trouble; then the desires become lusts or idols of the heart. When we have idols or *lusts of the heart*, it is as if those desires are the only things we can think about. It's like always having something in front of your face. When something is so close to your face, consuming your view, you see nothing else. Not God! Not others! Nothing but your own selfish desires.

Angela's Story

I am coming to believe that my clutter is an idol. I spend time thinking about what to do with it, moving it around, and getting rid of some of it. The bulk of my time is spent either worrying about my stuff or doing something with it. I worry about what to do with it, how to go about it, and, in short, obsessing over it.

I admit I'm materialistic. I'm so easily drawn into buying the promise of what the stuff can do for me that I don't think about what I may already have. In retrospect, I keep on buying and am never satisfied. Instead of a freeing life, the stuff has put me in prison, not only because of the way my home looks, but because I'm afraid to let others into my world for fear of judgment and condemnation.

My idol has all control over me, and I feel I can do nothing about it. I'm not sure why I feel this way, but I have been like this for as long as I can remember. Even my grandmother used to have several rooms in her home that she could not enter.

I feel these material goods have the ultimate power and authority over my life.

Then I remember that God has not given me a spirit of fear, but a spirit of power, love, and sound mind. But my reality of how I live suggests that I am someone who believes that fake treasures and unused possessions are my god.

I want my heart to be where God is. I want my body to be where God is. I want my desires to be only of God and His perfect will. I need to work diligently at letting go of all these idols and let God really come into my life. I keep pushing Him out by worrying about how to clean and restore order in my house. I need to always ask God to help me to get rid of the stuff. I need awareness that God does have a purpose for my life beyond getting rid of clutter and to make space for Him to reveal it.

Do you agree with Angela that clutter could become an idol? By "clutter" I mean, "the accumulation of objects that have lost their intended purpose."

For some people, clutter is an idol because their thoughts become focused on the stuff all day long. Their emotions are directly tied to the stuff, so their clutter becomes a safe haven that isolates them from others and God. The idol of clutter then becomes an all-consuming lifestyle.

Idols of the heart can develop in our lives from a very early age, or even generationally. We all know people who like to keep things for a "someday" need. In fact, many people born in the Great Depression era understandably have this mentality, but this lifestyle is based on fear instead of reason. Many times, this fear gets passed down from generation to generation. Some family members may dismiss it as irrational, but there are others within the family who pick up this mantle and continue the lifestyle, much to the concern of the family.

Perhaps you find yourself relating to Angela's story. If you do, then in order for you to understand this very complex issue, you'll need to answer two very important questions:

1. Looking back, can you remember when the clutter began to take over your home?

_____

_____

2. When did your clutter begin to erode your quality of life?

_____

_____

When life comes at us faster than we can think, most of us tend to accumulate clutter and become disorganized for a while. It happens to the best of us—a family member becomes ill, you may be hospitalized for an extended period, or you are assigned a project at work that requires a lot of travel. Your life changes. You move, get married, have kids, or start a new job. During times of transition, a certain amount of chaos, clutter, and disorganization is natural.

Situational Disorganization occurs when you find yourself in clutter or chaos for a short period of time, resulting from an unusual turn of events or changes in your life or living arrangements.

The Institute for Challenging Disorganization[30] defines Situational Disorganization as "a temporary state of disorganization caused by life circumstances."

To Think About

1. Have you experienced the death of a loved one or family member within the last six months?

_____

_____

2. Have you recently gone through a divorce?

_____

_____

3. Have you changed jobs or careers several times within the past year?

_____

_____

4. Have you recently moved to a new location?

_____

_____

5. Has a family member recently experienced a serious illness that occupies most of your waking hours, not permitting you to follow your previous routine that maintains order within your household?

_____

_____

6. Has a parent who is unable to care for himself/herself moved into your home?

_____

_____

7. Has the birth or adoption of a child upset the balance of your life more than you expected?

_____

_____

8. Have you experienced the "empty nest syndrome" in the past year?

_____

_____

Answering *yes* to any of these questions means there is a strong likelihood that you may experience Situational Disorganization as a result. Sometimes life happenings take our full attention, like a birth or a marriage. Overnight, you are thrown out of balance, but you figure that it is better to live with a messy house than to regret missing any of life's magnificent moments. At some point, most of us slowly settle in to a new normal. And while there is no roadmap showing us how to get back to a place of balance, in due time most of us get there.

For others, clutter in the home is normal. Maybe you were raised in an environment where life skills were not taught because everything was done for you, or you grew up having stuff all around and you see this as a normal expression of activity. Maybe your parents were *chronically disorganized*, or more intensely, you grew up in an abusive environment.

What Makes Chronic Disorganization Different?

According to the Institute for Challenging Disorganization, the definition of Chronic Disorganization is "having a past history of disorganization in which self-help efforts to change have failed, an undermining of current quality of life due to disorganization, and the expectation of future disorganization."[31] To paraphrase this, if you have tried to change this problem on your own but have failed, and if you believe most future attempts will have unsuccessful results, then you may suffer from Chronic Disorganization. Chronic Disorganization (CD) is not a matter of lack of willpower or weak character. These are chronic conditions that you can't overcome alone.

As Ariane Benefit clarifies, "The term 'chronically disorganized' is not a 'diagnosis' or an 'illness.' It is a 'trait' found in all kinds of people, at every income level." She and many other experts note that chronically disorganized people are often also highly functional, creative, intelligent, social, accomplished, energetic, enthusiastic, and fun to be with. She goes on to explain that this term is used to indicate that traditional organizing methods will probably not work and will require particularly unique and simple organizing solutions for the person to become more organized. This can include ongoing coaching to help change ingrained habits and sustain motivation, emotional support to increase self-confidence, and long-term support to maintain the organization skills.[32]

There are many reasons for the underlying conditions of CD individuals, and everyone is unique; however, there are generalities that can underlie some of the causes. Sometimes the underlying condition is neurologically based, such as attention deficit hyperactivity disorder (ADHD), traumatic brain injury (TBI), or other conditions such as fibromyalgia, chronic fatigue syndrome, or multiple sclerosis. There may be addiction or drug tendencies, compulsive saving, and the like, coupled with learning disorders like dyslexia, which can affect organization. Depression, anxiety disorders, or physical handicaps can also play a role.

The following chart will help you identify the difference between a situationally disorganized and chronically disorganized person.

Situational Disorganization	Chronic Disorganization
• Experienced a death of a loved one within the last six months • Recent divorce • Your home is used as a storage facility for short-term or uncertain length of time by a family or friend who is downsizing or experiencing a serious life transition • Job or career change several times within the past year • Sudden relocation of work results in moving • Family member's sickness requires your time, thus disrupting the time allocated to daily routine that maintains order within your household • Birth of a child or adoption of a child upset the balance of your life more than expected • Recent change to working from home, but have underestimated the required space	• Disorganization has been a factor in your life for many years • Disorganization interferes with the quality of your daily life or negatively affects your relations with others • Disorganization persists despite self-help attempts to get organized • Known as an "info maniac"; constantly saving many articles, newspapers, or books, read or unread • Accumulate possessions beyond apparent usefulness or pleasure • Desk, floor, and/or countertops covered in papers or objects that don't serve a purpose in that area • Felt deprived as a child, either emotionally or materially • Has wide range of interests and several uncompleted tasks and projects • Difficulty staying focused and easily distracted during tasks and projects • Tends to lose track of time

Someone could find themselves experiencing Chronic Disorganization for the first time as an adult. Parents or teachers may have served as a safety net while growing up, but they find that once on their own, the ability to stay organized is elusive. Trying to maintain some organization is simply not possible. Therefore, one is now faced with an eroding quality of life.

Author Peter Walsh says in *It's All Too Much*:

> Like so many people that I deal with . . . who you are and what you have are intimately linked. The things you buy, the item's value, the possessions you hoard are all a reflection of you, your life, your relationships, your career, and your aspirations. You are not your stuff, but believe me, your stuff reveals a great deal about who you are.[33]

Questions for Reflection:

1. Do you agree that clutter can become an idol? If so, in your own words, explain.

_____

_____

2. Looking at your particular circumstance, how do you classify your clutter? Are you Situationally Disorganized or Chronically Disorganized?

_____

_____

3. Why?

_____

_____

But I Just Wanted to Help!

Understanding the underlying cause of a cluttered lifestyle is paramount to the elimination process. Intervention from well-intended relatives who swoop in and interfere can actually cause more harm than good. Without proper education on the root causes, the CD client can become withdrawn, depressed, and even suicidal if changes are not within their control or their need for respect is not honored.

Organizers get countless calls from loving family members who want to help. However, the CD person does not often ask for this type of "help." CD individuals need more than a clearing out. They need the support of trained individuals who can help them uncover the causes for their beliefs. Once that is reasoned with, the clearing out process is one that takes minimal time and emotional toll.

How to Get Help for You or Your Loved One

To further explore Chronic Disorganization, consider working with a professional organizer and/or coach who specializes in this challenge. You can contact the Institute for Challenging Disorganization at www.challengingdisorganization.org.

The Institute for Challenging Disorganization will connect you with someone they have trained, or you may prefer to join a support group, either by phone or in person.

Lack of Follow-Through

For some, disorganization can be explained as simply as "not following through." The apostle Paul admonishes us in 2 Timothy 4:7 to "finish the race." In other words, to follow through with what you have started.

How many unfinished projects are on your hobby table? Finishing well takes discipline, and that's something that doesn't come naturally to most of us. Most of us are greatly energized at the beginning of a project. We see the end result in our mind's eye, dreaming of the wonderful outcome, but completing the task may take more time or demand more resources than we realized at the beginning.

This reminds me of the scripture James 2:22:

> You see that his faith and his actions were working together, and his faith was made complete by what he did.

It takes faith to believe that you will follow through; it takes your working at it to make it so! Glynnis Whitwer, author of *I Used to Be So Organized,* explains it like this:

> The good news is you can learn follow-through. Success with small, solid, disciplined habits leads to achievement with greater projects, which is why making your bed and being on time for church are important habits to master.[34]

God says that He will only entrust us with larger responsibilities if we have proven ourselves in the small ones first.

Clutter = Postponed Decisions

Sometimes your disorganization is not situational or chronic; it's just a result of life's ongoing demands that wear you out. Remember that clutter is nothing more than "postponed decisions."

> *Sometimes your disorganization is not situational or chronic; it's just a result of life's ongoing demands that wear you out.*

There are seasons in everyone's lives when we all just need to step back and reflect. Scarlett O'Hara, in *Gone with the Wind*, said it best: "I can't think about this right now. If I do, I'll go crazy. I'll think about that tomorrow."

I remember times when I was a new mother that just taking a shower was a monumental task. Some days I was too exhausted to make another decision, but delaying decisions always leads to disorganization. The piles of junk mail on the counter will multiply like rabbits when you delay making a decision about each piece. Realizing that no decision is ever perfect can help you decide what to do with it all. It's okay not to have *every* piece of information necessary to make a good decision. Even a bad decision is better than no decision, and most of the time you can change your course or direction if need be.

Scripture Study

Look up the following verses and write down what God says.

Psalm 115:4–8

_____

_____

Exodus 20:1–4

_____

_____

Revelation 9:20

_____

_____

1 John 2:15–17

_____

_____

What Will You Choose?

Clutter can manifest itself in many forms, and there are many reasons for it. We have a choice to make: Are we going to worship the things of this world, or are we going to worship the God who has created and authored these things? This is the same choice that Joshua gave the people of Israel at the end of his life. He said:

> Now fear the LORD and serve him with all faithfulness. Throw away the gods your ancestors worshiped beyond the Euphrates River and in Egypt, and serve the LORD. But if serving the LORD seems undesirable to you, then choose for yourselves this day whom you will serve, whether the gods your ancestors served beyond the Euphrates, or the gods of the Amorites, in whose land you are living. But as for me and my household, we will serve the LORD. (Joshua 24:14–15)

Are we going to worship the things of this world, or are we going to worship the God who has created and authored these things?

Organization Tip: Time Management Tips for Individuals or Households Affected by Chronic Disorganization from the Institute for Challenging Disorganization

Chronically disorganized individuals usually have a poor sense of time. They are often late for appointments and work, and their children are late for school. This often occurs because of their inability to find misplaced items and deal with distractions. They're also unrealistic about how long a task will take to complete.

The following are some ideas that will help with these issues as well as other time-saving tips.

Time Tips for Planning and Scheduling

- Plan your morning the night before.

Lay out the clothes you will wear; gather your briefcase and any items needed to take to work. Collect the children's clothes, backpacks, shoes, and items they will need to take to school and stage them in a convenient location. Think through everything you will need in the morning and have that ready to go. Request and encourage your school-age children to do this nightly to avoid morning madness.

- Find a place for your keys.

  A spot by the door or entry to your house makes a great place to hang or hold your keys. There are several ideas in catalogs, or you can find key holders in organizing stores. This space or area may also be a place where outgoing mail and other outgoing items are kept. A nice basket in the area works well.

- Schedule.

  Schedule your priority tasks early in the week so if they have to be postponed, there is still time left to complete them. Schedule the most difficult tasks during your "prime time" when you are at peak energy level.

- Assess your time.

  When planning errands, be realistic about the amount of time each errand will take. Add at least fifteen minutes to the time you think it will take. This way, you will learn not to overcommit and continually work under pressure.

- Create a message center.

  Maintain a family messaging center and a perpetual shopping list. Place your center in a location that is easily seen and accessible by everyone that will need to use it. There are hundreds of centers available to purchase either online or from your local office supply store. Remember to make it large enough to accommodate your growing family activities and needs.

- Give yourself realistic time frames.

  Recognize that you do not have to complete the entire job in one sitting. Do a little at a time by scheduling appointments with yourself and keeping them.

- Prioritize.

  Remember that you are procrastinating if you work on a trivial task while a more important one remains undone. Prioritize the jobs to be done and work on priorities first.[35]

Taking It to God

Father God,

Just the thought of praying to You about my constant disorganization is overwhelming. I have kept this idol in my life for so long, I'm not sure how I can begin to release it, but I know that You did not give me a spirit of fear, and that You will be with me because You will never forsake or leave me.

So, Father, I don't know why I keep trying to save everything. Maybe it's because of what I learned from my grandparents or parents who lived through the war times. They didn't have enough and sometimes they had nothing, and so they created many uses from the little that they owned. I know that I live in a different time now. I can try to understand them, appreciating what they tried to pass on to me, but I don't need to do what they did. I forgive myself for blindly trying to imitate their behavior. Even though I feel so guilty whenever I throw something out that could be used for something else, I give myself permission to let go of all the plastic containers, jars, and plastic bags from grocery stores. How many might I need, anyway?

I feel so ashamed to ask for help with my house because it's filled with all kinds of stuff—stuff only I can appreciate—stuff like clothes, toys, and papers that remind me of days long ago. I am so embarrassed that I can't even call a handyman to get the broken things fixed, and that makes everything worse.

Father, I need You to help me get help before everything gets worse. I pray You will direct my steps in finding the help I need. I am looking forward to the days when I can have guests over, but more than anything else, dear Lord, I need You to help me to stop bringing in more clutter. Father, I recognize that I have set stuff up on an idol altar.

Search my heart, expose the areas that brought me into this lifestyle, and let me cast out anything that keeps me from going forward. I forgive myself for waiting this long. I will remember that with Christ, all things are possible. I repent of making these false idols in my life. Amen.

Chapter 8
Taking the Land Using the Joshua Approach: Organizing One Step at a Time

You may say to yourselves, "These nations are stronger than we are. How can we drive them out?" But do not be afraid of them; remember well what the LORD your God did to Pharaoh and to all Egypt. You saw with your own eyes the great trials, the signs and wonders, the mighty hand and outstretched arm, with which the LORD your God brought you out. The LORD your God will do the same to all the peoples you now fear. Moreover, the LORD your God will send the hornet among them until even the survivors who hide from you have perished. Do not be terrified by them, for the LORD your God, who is among you, is a great and awesome God. The LORD your God will drive out those nations before you, little by little. You will not be allowed to eliminate them all at once, or the wild animals will multiply around you. But the LORD your God will deliver them over to you, throwing them into great confusion until they are destroyed.

Deuteronomy 7:17–23

Slow and Consistent Steps Make Lasting Changes

In Greek mythology, Sisyphus is condemned to push a huge stone to the top of a hill for all eternity. With great physical exertion, he pushes until the stone is at the top. He then immediately releases the stone and it rolls all the way back to the bottom again. Thus, his struggle is recognized as an "uphill battle."

Organizing may seem like that for many. You can spend an entire day, or maybe several exhausting days, organizing what may have taken weeks or years to create. At the end of your marathon, you are spent and weak from your efforts. What happens next? You "release" the stone and the next thing you know, things are once again in disarray.

It can be very discouraging to realize how long it takes to deal with clutter and how quickly clutter can collect again. The organizing process is very reminiscent of Sisyphus, isn't it? You start out working with great intensity, and once you release the boulder, your tendency is to relax, letting things go back to the familiar with no plan in place for maintenance.

Habits take time to reform in our brains. When we do too much too quickly, not only do we get exhausted and burned out for the next several days, but we can also undo all that we have accomplished. The initial organizing results look great, but you have to remember that keeping things looking that good is a matter of building daily habits—habits of organization.

It can be very discouraging to realize how long it takes to deal with clutter and how quickly clutter can collect again.

God promises that He will "drive out" with His mighty hand that which is keeping disorder in your life. But this can only happen as you "take the land," or the room! Building habits one at a time, little by little, will ensure great success and will make it possible for you to rule over your possessions instead of being ruled by them.

1. What do you think is "The Joshua Approach" to organizing your home and your schedule?

_____

_____

2. How does the caution, "You will not be allowed to eliminate them all at once, or the wild animals will multiply around you," apply to your life?

_____

_____

_____

_____

3. When have you attempted to do too much too quickly?

_____

_____

To Think About: Organizing Rules to Live By

1. Never buy more than you need.

   Bargains have a way of luring us into thinking we need to buy more because of a great price. Buying more than the space you have will result in clutter buildup.

2. When you buy one item, always dispose of two.

   When starting the decluttering process, remember that every time you buy something new, you'll need to train yourself to dispose of *two* articles that are like the new one coming in.

3. Build one habit at a time.

   Trying to develop six new habits at a time is a sure way to become overwhelmed. Don't let your desire to do it all at once ruin your efforts. I know many clients who have an all-or-nothing attitude. This attitude sets them up for exhaustion and failure before they even get started. *Yes*, you may backslide periodically, that's completely normal. However, if you have taken measures to "keep the wild beasts away," getting organized again will only take half the time and effort as your original endeavor.

Amy's Story

Please remember that your home didn't get into this shape at the rate of one room per day, and it's not going to get out of this shape at the rate of one room per day either. Sure, you can continue to purge at that rate, but when you're done, you won't even remember what you got rid of, where you put the things you kept, or even what you kept. Trust me, I know.

I purged my sewing room very quickly within the past few months, and now there are things that I either can't find or wish I had never gotten rid of.

Sure, I had good reason to get rid of a lot of stuff, but there are items that I now wish I'd kept, because I've gone looking for them and have come to the conclusion that they were among the purged items.

Fighting for Your Land

God told Joshua He would give His people the land, but that didn't mean they could just stand there and expect the land to be handed over to them without their part in the taking.

Fighting for what you want takes a plan, commitment, and strength. Your land is not going to be handed over to you. The question is, are you willing to fight for it? It's easy to just sit and delay and continue to pile. It's easy to accept less than what God wants for you. It's easy to back down from fights and never take the land God wants for you because you don't want to face the clutter giants.

Work and think your way through the following organizing principles, especially as you begin to "take the land" in your home.

Organizing Action Plan:

1. Pray.

   Nothing can replace the power of prayer. By allowing God to be part of your organizing session, you will be open to new concepts that otherwise would have gone unnoticed. Also, ask for intercessory prayer from friends and family. Order is of God, and you are seeking *His* will as you begin this new process.

2. Plan your work.

   Winging it will lead to frustration. Plan your time and schedule and what you want to actually accomplish during your session. Here are some example questions to get you started on your plan:

   - What is the vision for this space?
   - What items fit that vision and what does not?
   - Where do I want to start?
   - Do I have all the tools necessary to organize? If not, what's missing?
   - Did I tell everyone I am not to be disturbed?
   - Did I remember to bring in water to keep hydrated during the project?

- Do I have enough music for the time I need to spend on this space?
- What steps have I taken to ensure that the "wild beast" (clutter) will not come creeping back?

3. Decide how long you want your organizing sessions to last.

   Remember that clutter is the result of postponed decisions. Organizing is not only physically challenging, but mentally draining as well. You now have to make decisions that you have postponed for a long, long time. Sessions lasting longer than three to four hours can completely wear you out. When you have had a couple of these sessions, you will be able to gauge how much of the land can be taken per session. The clutter didn't accumulate overnight, so it will take time to get the room under control again. Watch the time!

4. Keep distractions at bay.

   Make a house rule that you are not to be disturbed during your sessions either by phone calls, the doorbell, or family members asking for help. This is *your* time to focus on the task at hand.

5. Keep hydrated and wear loose clothing.

   Keeping your body hydrated will help you maintain your mental focus. Wearing appropriate clothing will make organizing more comfortable.

6. Stay encouraged!

   In the middle of your organizing session, you may feel as if the room looks worse than when you started. Yes, it can be disheartening to realize that as you begin the organizing process, your room looks like a war zone. Take heart, it will all come together in the end if you have a plan and stick to it. Developing a plan for each session will ensure your daily successes, even if it doesn't look like it!

7. Delegate.

   Are there organizing tasks you find difficult to do? Is that large piece of furniture not only in the way, but no longer a part of the vision you have for the space? Enlist the help of a friend, family member, or local junk guy to help you remove it. Delegate when you can.

8. Maintain.

The key to continuing with your organizing efforts is to build a maintenance schedule into your system. Find someone to help keep you accountable until

> *The key to continuing with your organizing efforts is to build a maintenance schedule into your system.*

the maintenance is routine. If you get into the habit of scheduling a short end-of-the-day decluttering session, things will remain more orderly all the time. This will ensure that you won't find yourself in the same disorganization as before.

Many of my clients have told me, "This is just too hard for me!" In our quest to achieve order in our homes, many of us have given up too soon because the effort seems too hard. It's easy to feel as if we may never be able to change old habits!

In many ways, the journey is just as important as the destination. God desires for us to grow from our struggles. The life lessons learned as we gain order in our homes will become positive habits that will enable us to transform our entire lifestyle.

Which of the eight organizing principles is hardest for you to follow?

_____

_____

Scripture Study

Look up the following verses and answer the question.

Deuteronomy 8:1–9
How does this passage remind you to take care of *your* land?

_____

_____

Organizing Tip: A Very Good Place to Start

Begin decluttering with this method:

1. Subdivide your room into small areas and then choose one area where you will begin to organize. Bring four bins or containers to the area.

   • Label bin #1 "Keep."

- Label bin #2 "Trash."
- Label bin #3 "Take Someplace Else."
- Label bin #4 "Give Away."

2. As you begin the sorting process, put each item into one of the four bins. Are you going to keep it? Then put it into the "Keep" bin. Do you want to donate it? Then put it into the "Donate" bin. The key here is to not move from the area or what I call the "circle of work." Taking a bathroom item into the bathroom will disrupt the process and distract you from your work area. Put your "Take Someplace Else" item into that bin. Keep your focus on that area until everything is completed. Then move to either the left or to the right and continue to sweep the entire room in a systematic process. Distractions occur when we zigzag in our decluttering because we feel it necessary to put things away immediately. In doing so, we forget what we were doing.

Taking It to God

Lord,

Thank You for opening my eyes up to Your promise that You will drive out the clutter beasts from my life. Thank You for showing me that I need to build new habits, little by little. Your Son, Jesus, said, "My yoke is easy." Remind me of that when things get hard again.

I never understood why I spent countless hours taking the "land of my room" only to be discouraged again because the wild beasts came back in and devoured all I had done. I now know I have to take it easy, do it bit-by-bit, and create and maintain a schedule to keep it that way. Thank You that I can rely on Your help as I move toward changing old habits. Thank You that You are the One who will help me transform my lifestyle. Amen.

Chapter 9

Like Paper, Like Manna:
Conquering Paper Clutter through Trust

Trust in the LORD with all your heart, and lean not on your own understanding; in all your ways acknowledge Him, and He shall direct your paths.

Proverbs 3:5–6 NKJV

Papers, papers everywhere . . . and not a place to write! For all our dreams of a paperless lifestyle, paper is still the number one culprit of disorganization . . . go figure!

If you're afraid to clear the paper clutter off your desktop or kitchen counter because you feel that putting the papers away will make you forget about them, you're not alone! The thought of throwing out information found in newspapers, catalogs, and magazines causes more anxiety than discarding other objects in our homes. There are three fears that lead to paper clutter.

1. Decision making.

    I have found that by far, decision making is the number one fear. This inability to make decisions causes clutter!

2. General fear of scarcity.

    We fear the thought that we will need something one day, so we keep it all (IRS returns, bills, contracts, bank statements, etc.). Paper

> *The thought of throwing out information found in newspapers, catalogs, and magazines causes more anxiety than discarding other objects in our homes.*

holds a lot of important information that we are afraid of losing. I have a client that fears the loss of electricity or computer access, so she creates all her documents in duplicate!

3. Retrieval problem.

   Because we fear losing paper in a file or pile, we end up making lots of little special piles for our special papers.

What is the antidote for this fear?

Trust!
In Exodus 16:4, 17–19 God speaks to Moses:

"I will rain down bread from heaven for you. The people are to go out each day and gather enough for that day." . . . The Israelites did as they were told; some gathered much, some little. . . . Everyone had gathered just as much as they needed. Then Moses said to them, "No one is to keep any of it until morning."

Manna was the tiny honey-tasting wafers the Israelites ate that was chock-full of minerals and vitamins. What had God asked His children to do? To only gather what they needed for that day. However, some of them paid no attention to Moses; they kept part of the manna until morning, but it spoiled and was useless to them. If they hoarded or stored extra, what happened? It spoiled.

Manna Lessons for Today

- Gather what you need.
- Share what you can.
- Don't hoard.
- Give away the excess = less clutter.

To Think About

You'd think that the Israelites—who saw God's hand in their deliverance and many miracles escaping the Egyptians—would have no problem trusting God to continue to deliver them into the promised land. But we know that trust was not in their hearts. They continued to harass Moses and complain that their provisions were not satisfying.

Trust didn't come naturally to them, nor does it come naturally to us. Most of us would rather trust in our own abilities than seek God for His provisions and direction. However, God's lesson for His children regarding trust was as true then as it is today. Think about paper information as being like manna. The sad fact is that paper has a very short shelf life. Ideally, information gathered on paper will end up in the recycling bin when the information is no longer needed. But the reality is that many of us hoard information because we think, *I may need this someday.* Information, or the perceived power that knowledge brings, is why most people keep paper.

One of my students said that she kept many papers because she believed that one day someone might need them and she would look stupid for not keeping them if she tossed them. As she articulated her thoughts, she confronted the lies that her self-worth was rooted in her papers.

> *Information, or the perceived power that knowledge brings, is why most people keep paper.*

There is more to paper than just the print. Paper holds vast emotional attachments and personal value because it represents significance. We think, *If I have this piece of paper, then I will have the knowledge. Even if I haven't read it, I still can someday.*

For many of us, paper piles erode our ability to function. Paper piles begin to creep onto the kitchen or dining room tables, making it impossible to have a family meal. If you are missing out on quality family time at dinner because of hurried schedules and/or a poor paper-management system, then eventually, the family structure will begin to suffer. The piles can obstruct our hallways, making it a hazard to walk up and down the stairs. I've witnessed several clients who have been rushed to the ER because of a fall due to paper piles.

Simply stated, paper-management problems are trust-in-God issues. The Israelites had to *trust* God to supply their needs on a daily basis. We need to cultivate that same level of trust so we can begin to let go of the paper piles that clog our ability to function. We need to believe that we can really trust God to meet our information needs

---

Paper holds vast emotional attachments and personal value because it represents significance. "If I have this piece of paper, then I will have the knowledge. Even if I haven't read it, I still can someday."

---

on an "as needed" basis. God supplied the Israelites with their day-to-day provisions. Not trusting God to meet our daily needs allows worry and anxiety to fill our souls.

Scripture Study

Look up the following verses and answer the questions.

Matthew 6:25–27, John 14:27, and Philippians 4:6–7
What does God say about worrying?

_____

_____

Philippians 4:19, Matthew 6:8, Psalm 34:10, and Romans 8:32
What does God say about our needs?

_____

_____

The Problem May Be . . . Tactile Sympathy

In her book *What Every Professional Organizer Needs to Know about Chronic Disorganization*, author Judith Kolberg defines this theory called Tactile Sympathy. Kolberg writes:

> I notice that when my clients touch a piece of clothing or loose piece of paper, and then are asked if they want to throw it away, their response is rarely to discard that item. If, however, I hold the garment or document and ask them whether or not to discard it, the chances of discarding improve by over 50 percent.[36]

Based on my own observation, this theory has been proven countless times. God has given us incredible tactile sensory abilities, and somehow, they are connected to our emotions. Clients rarely want to part with something they are emotionally connected with.

Remember that it may take only a fraction of a second when handling a piece of paper to develop an attachment. If you find you have difficulty throwing out paper and such, enlist the help of a friend, spouse, or professional organizer to hold up the items. You may find you can come to a decision faster without handling the objects.

Another wonderful tip is to wear cleaning gloves. If you find yourself alone in your organizing sessions, wearing these gloves will put a barrier between your tactile tips and the object's sensory output. I've had several clients tell me how delighted they were to see this in their own experiences.

"It's nothing less than a miracle," one stated.

Organizing Tip: Make Piles of Papers and Magazines Disappear

1. Reduce junk mail.

   It's not the mailman's fault! Stop the junk mail from coming into your home forever. You can fight back. There are many services on the internet to help you eliminate junk mail. Some provide a free service. It will only cost you the time of recording unwanted catalogs and other unwanted mail. I would write here a list of the many services you can join; however, they change so frequently that by the time this is published many will no longer be useful. Keep checking the internet to find the latest and *best* companies for this service. It is time well spent!

2. Give your papers a home.

   Many times paper piles accumulate because they have no home. Current papers that come into the home such as bills, upcoming events, children's permission slips, items that need to be ordered, or papers that need reviewing for decisions are just a few categories for incoming papers. Others could include receipts and tax documents for the current year, warranties for new items, health information, or home maintenance records. Set up a filing system where these important papers can be placed and easily accessed.

3. What to do with your vital records.

   In an emergency, you need to be able to grab these precious documents or you need a safe place to house these documents. Trying to replace them can cause a huge headache, so it's best to be proactive and set up a system for these important records as soon as possible. These include, but aren't limited to, birth, wedding, and death certificates, passports, Social Security cards, wills, and savings bonds.

O-H-I-O: Only Handle It Once

Clutter happens when we delay deciding what to do with the paper piles. The first thing to do is to establish a routine for handling the daily papers. Setting up a center where you keep a shredder and recycling bin nearby will help in completing your daily paper task. Practice the art of O-H-I-O. Handle each paper on top before moving to the paper underneath. Keep both hands free instead of looking at your papers with one hand. Decide the action for each paper before moving to the next.

Desktop File for Action Items

Give papers that require timely action a home by using a desktop filing system. A desktop file can be purchased at The Container Store (www.thecontainerstore.com) or at your favorite office product store. Their main purpose is to keep all action-oriented files in one neat and accessible place so that you aren't hunting for papers beneath mountains of piles.

For example: If you have five envelopes in your mailbox—two are bills, one is an invitation for a birthday party, one is a school-related item for your daughter, and one goes to your husband for review—you can quickly organize them with your desktop system.

Set up a file labeled for each category. The bills will be housed in your bill folder, your upcoming event will be housed in a folder called "Events," your daughter's school information will be housed in a folder with her name on it. Any information needing your husband's attention will be housed in his folder with his name. Remember, these are *not* resource files, but an action system that is to contain only those things that are action-oriented or those things that need your immediate attention.

My clients create what I call a "red-hot folder" for any action that must be completed within a twenty-four- to forty-eight-hour period. The key is to remember to use your system every day. This maintains the inflow and output of your folders, ensuring that your items receive daily attention.

Warranties and Instructions

Most of my clients have bulging file cabinets because their warranty and instruction manuals are placed there. I recommend getting a file tote instead. Find a decorative tote in which you can customize the labels. Go room by room and find all the items that have warranty information. For example: In your den you may have a TV, stereo equipment, a DVD player, and gaming equipment. Label a section in your tote "Den."

File all warranty and instruction information for each product under the specific room, not under the item's name. A filing system works well when information is easily accessible and retrievable. Manufacturers are getting very smart. They are now listing their warranties and instructions on the web. How wonderful to know that if we didn't save something, or if we can't find the instructions to a particular product, all we have to do is search the internet, and there it is!

Sentimental Papers

Yes, we all have them. If you're like me, you love to keep birthday cards, love notes from your spouse, or drawings from a child. Those items hold precious memories. Creating a display of these in a frame or shadow box will add personality to your home. It also says that you honor and respect those precious memories when you share them with others.

However, if you don't have room or just want to store them, make sure the box is acid-free and tucked away in a dark, climate-controlled area. Remember to date and make notes on the back of these papers: Include who they are from and any special notes to explain why they mean so much to you.

Within the past few decades, our world has changed in paper consumption. We now rely more heavily on electronic information. You'd think our paper piles would have decreased, and in some respects, they have. However, we are still attached to keeping paper backups, and the paper piles have remained. In addition to our paper piles, we now have electronic clutter such as emails, internet information, and the like. Our organizing needs have doubled! But there are things you can do about it.

Sign up for online statements, and scan and store information electronically.

Paying bills and reviewing statements online saves paper and time. This is an ecologically sound and secure way to reduce the amount of paper in your home.

Another option is to scan older documents if you still want to reference them, and then keep them electronically, plus a backup copy. Your backup could be a CD, flash drive, external hard drive, or cloud backup. There are many free cloud services you can sign up for, and some that have a minimal cost. The peace of mind you have in knowing that if your computer crashes, your documents are safe, is priceless. Plus, you can access a service from any computer with an internet connection. Identity theft is a serious problem, so many shy away from using online services for this reason. My advice is to educate yourself about the risks and benefits. Become an expert in safe internet practices, and your confidence will increase as you make decisions based on fact, not fear.

The Seven Information Management Questions™

1. What information do I need to keep?

    _____

    _____

2. In what form?

    _____

    _____

3. For how long?

    _____

    _____

4. Who is responsible for filing it?

    _____

    _____

5. Who needs access to it?

    _____

    _____

6. How can I find it?

    _____

    _____

7. How is it backed up?

    _____

    _____

Questions for Reflection:

Think about the present paper situation in your home and work through the following questions:

Why do you want to get your papers organized?

_____

_____

What is the benefit to getting your papers organized?

_____

_____

Does everyone in the family understand why you are doing this?

_____

_____

How can you keep junk mail from coming into your home?

_____

_____

Where is the best place to keep the papers that you are currently working on?

_____

_____

How can you make sure that you will work on your paper piles every day?

_____

_____

How much information is needed in order for you to make a decision?

_____

_____

Can you really trust God to direct you to what is needed on a daily basis?

_____

_____

Taking It to God

Lord,

    I now believe that my paper piles are truly a reflection of my lack of trust. I have taken on a self-sufficiency attitude in which I must be in control of my decisions, gathering much information in order to make the best decisions. I have forgotten to trust You to help me make the right choices in my life. Forgive me, Father, as I repent of my old ways. Help me to renew my thinking, because I now trust in You. I now trust Your guidance and know that You love me so much that no problem is too trivial for You. Show me what is truly essential to keep, and teach me to discern true value. I am learning that life is simply too big for me to handle alone. No matter how good the information or advice seems to be, if it isn't consistent with what You have told me through Your Word, it is not to be trusted. I will trust in You, Lord, and lean not on my own understanding . . . God, You are in control . . . even in the paper details! Amen.

Chapter 10
Teach Me to Number My Days

O LORD, *make me know my end and what is the measure of my days; let me know how fleeting I am! Behold, you have made my days a few handbreadths, and my lifetime is as nothing before you. Surely all mankind stands as a mere breath! Selah.*

Psalm 39:4–5 ESV

Time is free, but it's priceless. You can't own it, but you can use it. You can't keep it, but you can spend it. Once you've lost it you can never get it back.

—Harvey MacKay

Our society today is so into microwaving, we have forgotten that God is into marinating. He wants to get inside of us, not just get us cooking.

We move and think at breakneck speed. Digital clocks, dinner in less than thirty minutes, sound bites for important world issues. It's no wonder we forget to stop and breathe during the day.

A dear friend has a wonderful way of stopping. When she is driving and comes to a stop sign, she actually stops (really . . . I know . . . hard to believe) and she counts to three. She takes a deep breath, thanks God, and asks for protection to wherever she needs to go, and then can concentrate on the here and now. She has also learned the art of prioritizing (I know why she is a great friend of mine).

How does having a disorganized environment impact our time?

Have you noticed that when your space is cluttered you spend needless hours, virtually every day, looking for lost items, such as keys, money, shoes, tools, etc.? Even when we're looking right at the lost item, it becomes difficult to see when surrounded by *clutter*. All that time adds up!

Not only does one lose valuable time searching for misplaced items, but clutter has a way of occupying our minds so that we waste time mulling over our list of what to do. Clutter not only occupies three-dimensional spaces, but the dimension of time is often affected by the space we occupy.

We can get so caught in the web of our world that we forget our own priorities. It is God who has given us our daily tasks. Just because we can do "X" doesn't mean He called us to do "X." How do we know the difference? We need to listen. How do we hear? We need to spend time getting quiet, listening to our hearts, listening to His words. When taking the time to breathe at the shore, in the meadows, or even on a soccer field, then we will know what He has called us to do.

When have you heard that still, small voice?

I just love it when I get an idea and I have absolutely no idea why I thought of it. I chuckle knowing that it wasn't my thought. Many of those thoughts center on the need to call a certain someone or to pray for my neighbor. God's list is always simple. It's only one or two meaningful tasks. But I know *I* didn't have them on my to-do list. That's our priority, to listen to the small, still voice. What if today's action really counts for tomorrow? Remember, we are all given the same amount of time in a day. What and how we honor that which has been so freely given can prosper us.

Does the way you manage your time reflect what's important to you? In light of the sudden COVID deaths, many us are rethinking how short life can be.

> O Lord, make me know my end and what is the measure of my days; let me know how fleeting I am! Behold, you have made my days a few handbreadths, and my lifetime is as nothing before you. Surely all mankind stands as a mere breath! Selah. (Psalm 39:4–5 ESV)

It's humbling to read this Psalm, because we know all too well the reality of how truly short our time and influence is on this earth. I take great consolation that we have eternity to look forward to, but I also know that our eternity will be measured by how well we choose to use the time God entrusts us with. (Remember the "To Be Ready" in the introduction?)

It would seem that the concept of time has been illusive throughout the ages, as the Bible is replete with many passages admonishing us to use our time wisely. Isn't it interesting that the world is obsessed with getting more done in the shortest amount of time; no wonder time-management books rank high on bestseller lists.

Begin at the Very Beginning:

- Productivity versus priorities.

Time is one thing money can't buy. And while we each have the same twenty-four hours every day, some of us are a lot more productive with them. How we spend our time says a lot about our priorities and our habits.

- Recognize your strengths.

God has given to each of us giftings and talents, and when we recognize our particular strengths, it becomes clear that there are things only we can do, so we would do well to delegate the rest to those able to do a better job in less time.

- Concentrate on your gift.

When we concentrate on our giftings and allow others to excel in theirs, our time seems to be quadrupled. We waste so much time thinking we need to do everything; we do so because we think our way is the best way.

> For we are God's [own] handiwork (His workmanship), recreated in Christ Jesus, [born anew] that we may do those good works which God predestined (planned beforehand) for us [taking paths which He prepared ahead of time], that we should walk in them [living the good life which He prearranged and made ready for us to live]. (Ephesians 2:10 AMPC)

- Tap into your intuition.

Oh, those precious and few days when we can say, "I was there just at the right time." Tapping into our intuition to be at a certain place at an opportune moment takes more than mere happenstance. If you are truly honest with yourself, you'll realize that such moments were usually planned, and free from distractions, which allowed you to concentrate on being in the here and now.

- Be fully engaged.

Being fully engaged—not wondering if you're going to make it on time to an appointment, or upset because the day isn't moving at a manageable flow—doesn't just happen. Being fully engaged can be realized when we plan out our days by padding our time. By planning your day and padding the time between your scheduled events, you have given yourself room to breathe and fully live in the present. Your ability to accomplish what was purposed for the day is the result of being fully engaged in the activity of the moment.

Here's a snapshot of what was just explained:

Make a list of the things, people, relationships, activities, habits, etc. that you say are a priority in your life. Now look at the last few weeks or months of your life, at what you do day in and day out. Do they reflect what's important to you? What will you commit to changing?

Sarah's Story

Last Sunday was my first Sunday back to church since the shutdown because of COVID. *Everyone* in church was weeping during service because we were so very grateful to be in the presence of each other and feeling the glory of God within our church.

Most of us recognized that time is not on our side. The precious gatherings that we took for granted are ones to be treasured. So I was awestruck by the concept of time and how much I truly have left to do what God has called me to.

I took your course several years ago and what stood out to me was the "to be ready" reason for getting my home and mind free of clutter. Since we don't know the hour or day of our return home or His return to us, it is now more critical than ever to recognize the need to bring God's order, by *Get Organized God's Way*, into my life. I have done several projects little by little, but I still have some major rooms to do. I now will put on the full armor and begin with God's direction on completing that which I have started.

Thank you again for putting the words down on paper, which God has given to you and in such a timely manner. Our time is indeed fleeting, and His order only allows us to be directed on the path He has planned for us. May God richly bless you.

Scripture Study
Read the following verses and write down what God says:

He has made everything beautiful in its time. He has also set eternity in the human heart; yet no one can fathom what God has done from beginning to end. (Ecclesiastes 3:11)

_____

_____

As long as it is day, we must do the works of him who sent me. Night is coming, when no one can work. (John 9:4)

_____

_____

Teach us to number our days, that we may gain a heart of wisdom. (Psalm 90:12)

_____

_____

But about that day or hour no one knows, not even the angels in heaven, nor the Son, but only the Father. Be on guard! Be alert! You do not know when that time will come. (Mark 13:32–33)

_____

_____

There is a time for everything, and a season for every activity under the heavens: a time to be born and a time to die, a time to plant and a time to uproot, a time to kill and a time to heal, a time to tear down and a time to build, a time to weep and a time to laugh, a time to mourn and a time to dance, a time to scatter stones and a time to gather them, a time to embrace and a time to refrain from embracing, a time to search and a time to give up, a time to keep and a time to throw away, a time to tear and a time to mend, a time to be silent and a time to speak, a time to love and a time to hate, a time for war and a time for peace. (Ecclesiastes 3:1–8)

_____

_____

Yet you do not know what tomorrow will bring. What is your life? For you are a mist that appears for a little time and then vanishes. (James 4:14 ESV)

_____

_____

And let us not grow weary of doing good, for in due season we will reap, if we do not give up. (Galatians 6:9 ESV)

But I trust in you, O LORD; I say, "You are my God." My times are in your hand. (Psalm 31:14–15 ESV)

Time is your most precious gift, because you only have a set amount of it. —Rick Warren

Serve God by doing common actions in a heavenly spirit, and then, if your daily calling only leaves you cracks and crevices of time, fill them up with holy service. —Charles Spurgeon

Oswald Chambers says in *My Utmost for His Highest*:

Don't plan without God. God seems to have a delightful way of upsetting the plans we have made, when we have not taken Him into account. We get ourselves into circumstances that were not chosen by God, and suddenly we realize that we have been making our plans without Him—that we have not even considered Him to be a vital, living factor in the planning of our lives. . . . In spiritual issues it is customary for us to put God first, but we tend to think that it is inappropriate and unnecessary to put Him first in the practical, everyday issues of our lives. If we have the idea that we have to put on our "spiritual face" before we can come near to God, then we will never come near to Him. We must come as we are.[37]

This is what the LORD says . . . , "Forget the former things; do not dwell on the past. See, I am doing a new thing! Now it springs up; do you not perceive it? I am making a way in the wilderness and streams in the wasteland." (Isaiah 43:16, 18–19)

How To Honor God with Simple Time Management Tips

Before the day even begins, acknowledge your Father in heaven. It's imperative so your focus is on the priorities that reflect the most important things in your life.

The following are a few tried-and-true time-management tips to help your days and life become more productive and life fulfilling:

1. Set a timer.

    Whether it is an alarm clock, cell phone, computer, or timer, set it at least thirty minutes prior to when you need to leave. Too often we fall prey to distractions or the "it will just take a few more minutes" syndrome, which ends with us being late.

2. Write down your to-do or appointment list the night before.

    We are more likely to follow through when we write things down, and even more so when we do it in advance. This simple action submits our "to-dos" to our subconscious memory. This is also my prayer time at the end of the day to review and to seek the actions for the next day.

3. Set up reminders.

    Find a great app for your computer or cell phone that will ring to help remind you of your daily tasks and to keep you on schedule.

4. Give up the cape.

    Chances are, you are not a superhero. Learn the art of saying "No." Concentrate on what is important in your life now. Begin to let go of activities and people that drain your energies and mental happiness. Time-management experts and philosophers are fond of reminding us that our time *is* our life. Whatever controls our time, controls our life.

5. Find accountability partners.

    Share your new time-management goals with your friends, family, and coworkers. Accountability is a strong motivator; if you know people are watching and are going to be there for you, that extra little push may make all the difference. Encouragement from those we care about motivates us to accomplish what we would fail to do on our own.

6. Schedule time with yourself, without interruptions.

   If that means closing your door and letting go of instant messages, then that's what you need to do. Do this at your most productive time of the day. Are you a morning person? Start your day out with some quiet time by yourself, when you're the most productive and focused.

7. Don't multitask.

   That's right! These days, people have found that they're much more productive when they're allowed to focus on one task at a time, rather than constantly juggling a dozen different projects at once. Think about it—don't you feel like you've actually accomplished something when you can cross things off your list?

8. Slow down to hear from God.

   Does it seem like everyone and everything is vying for your attention all at once? It can be hard for us to know what to do first, let alone try to find the time to get caught up.

For we are God's [own] handiwork (His workmanship), recreated in Christ Jesus, [born anew] that we may do those good works which God predestined (planned beforehand) for us [taking paths which He prepared ahead of time], that we should walk in them [living the good life which He prearranged and made ready for us to live]. (Ephesians 2:10 AMPC)

The Bible says that what we do will be tested:

Now if anyone builds on the foundation with gold, silver, precious stones, wood, hay, straw—each one's work will become manifest, for the Day will disclose it, because it will be revealed by fire, and the fire will test what sort of work each one has done. If the work that anyone has built on the foundation survives, he will receive a reward. If anyone's work is burned up, he will suffer loss, though he himself will be saved, but only as through fire. (1 Corinthians 3:12–15 ESV)

May your time be filled with the activities that bring you immense joy and purpose. May you do what you love and love what you do with time enough to spare.

Questions for Reflection:

1. Why do you hurry to get things done?

_____

_____

2. If your hurriedness grants you some extra time, how do you use it?

_____

_____

Family?

_____

_____

Self?

_____

_____

Community?

_____

_____

God?

_____

_____

3. How can you apply better time management into your life?

_____

_____

4. What is your first priority?

_____

_____

5. In what ways does clutter interrupt time with God?

_____

_____

Taking It to God

Dear Lord God,

You are the Alpha and the Omega. You know the beginning from the end. All the days of the earth are in Your hands and everyone who has ever been born was so born for such a time as this.

How do we truly learn to measure the days of our lives? Time is such a fleeting concept, because once it is gone, it can never be retrieved, no matter how much we may want to travel back in time. Father, teach me to measure the days left of my life. These recent pandemic years have brought the world to a standstill, and many I know have learned to readjust their time and slow down. How I envy them. I guess I was never taught those skills, and my days just seem to run into each other. I now understand to start my day seeking Your purpose for my day. Measuring the important versus the minor details and deciding on a new importance is key. Your purpose supersedes my need to fill my days.

"Seek ye first the kingdom of God" starts with learning to give You the time. My choices today do have consequences for my tomorrows. I pray that I can hear Your small voice as I redeem my space and create more time in my life for those that are closest to me.

It was strange to observe that the more cluttered my environment became; the more time was wasted in getting things done. Now that I am on this journey to establish order in my home, I find that my time has increased. You are a God of order and of time. May Your blessings continue to unfold every day. In Jesus's name, Amen.

Chapter 11

How to Organize Anything: Let All Things Be Done Decently and in Order

But everything should be done in a fitting and orderly way.
1 Corinthians 14:40

Over the past few chapters, I have challenged you to look deeply into God's divine order and His desire for your life. I have also given you a blueprint to build new thinking processes and priorities. In doing so, I have increased the probability that your future organized space can become a reality. But more importantly, it will be one that is *maintained*.

The next few pages are not an attempt to teach you every "how-to" organizing possibility you may encounter on your journey, but to get you on the path to a better-organized future.

Anyone who has tried to get organized knows it can be tough. But while organizing your life can be tricky, it's interesting to note why some attempts succeed while others fail.

The demands placed on organizer services have increased since COVID entered our way of life in 2020. Many organizers chose to go the virtual route in helping clients. A few months after the surges in COVID, demand increased because our society saw the need for a better-organized environment, since more people now work from home and more time is spent in our home environments.

Thankfully, the skills needed to become better organized both in terms of physical space and time *can* be taught. Getting organized requires a well-thought-out plan, a realistic time frame, determination, and a skill set and knowledge base to accomplish your goals. But for the long-term, *getting* organized is really not the problem, *staying* organized is. Staying organized is not about what you did to alphabetize the spice rack; it's about what you *believe* and what you *think*.

> *Staying organized is not about what you did to alphabetize the spice rack; it's about what you believe and what you think.*

You will notice that this chapter is formatted a little differently from the others. That's because we're going to get to the nitty-gritty of actual organization techniques. The entire chapter will be devoted to vital organizational tips that will help you with your organized lifestyle. So let's get started!

Beginning at the Beginning

I just love the quote "Ready . . . Fire . . . Aim!" Many people seem to follow this for their organizing processes. They get hooked into the latest "big" thing on the market without analyzing the process or developing their plan. Talk about wasted time and money! So let's get started with the right approach:

Ready . . . (That is, plan.)
Aim . . . (Decide on your course of action for this session, making sure all tools for the task are with you.)
Fire . . . (Get started!)

To Think About

1. What is your vision for the space?

   Create a strategy that works with your lifestyle. Organizing isn't about how a space looks; it's about how a space *functions*. Analyze the situation before you attack! When creating a vision for your space, ask yourself the following questions:

   • What activities will you do in this space? The more activities in a confined area, the more clutter.

- What items no longer meet the criteria for those activities? (Look around the area.) I liken this to a sculpture. Take out everything that doesn't belong with that vision.

2. How much time will it take?

   Time is not definable. The only thing we know about time is that it moves forward. Everyone has his or her own concept of time, and that's when we get into trouble when deciding to organize. As novices, we either underestimate or overestimate how much time an activity will take. For example, you can look at your closet and figure out that it can take you two hours to complete the task of deciding what stays and what can be donated. In two hours, you can either be completely finished or be only half done. It all depends on how fast you can make decisions and how deeply you want to go in the organizing process, not to mention how many distractions happen during the two hours. Never bite off more than you can chew. Develop a plan *before* you begin. Break down the tasks into bite-size pieces. By having a beginning-middle-and-end strategy in mind, you will be well equipped to complete the job. When you come to the end of one part of the process, you will not have to feel that everything has to be done right away.

Vision without action is a dream. Action without vision is simply passing the time. Action with vision is making a positive difference. —Joel Barker[38]

We live in a digital age. Most of our clocks are digital, so unfortunately, we have forgotten how long the passage of time takes. How long is ten minutes? Most people don't have a clue as to what can be done in this short period of time.

I explain that we need to strengthen our time muscle. I ask my clients to set their minute timer to ten minutes. Then, I have them work on a small area and not stop until the bell rings. When focused on a specific task, most are amazed at how much can be done in a small amount of time. After several repeated sessions, they become clear about what they can and cannot accomplish. It's very important that you understand the passage of time so that your goals can be completed.

Alice's Story of Determination

Yesterday, I determined that I needed to be able to use my entire closet. Always in the past, when I have tackled any organizing project, it has seemed like it looked worse afterward than when I began. I always pull everything out and get completely overwhelmed, and even though I might get close to finishing, I never actually finish.

This time, however, it was different. Armed with the knowledge that I must not pull out more than I could deal with effectively, and that I absolutely must not quit until I had accomplished my goal, *I did it*. I determined that all I wanted to do was to make a path to the other side of the closet. I pulled out just a little and dealt with it as I went along. I just kept plugging along until I got the area looking nice. It was highly motivating, and I really hated to stop and go to bed!

Scripture Study

Read Galatians 6:9. Why is it so important to not give up as you begin to get your life in order?

_____

_____

From Dreams to Reality . . . Getting It Done

Step 1: Eliminate the excess before you organize.

Let's reexamine chapter one, identifying what you treasure.

Keeping your treasures front and center, both earthly and heavenly, will be a critical step in allowing you to identify what is truly important in your current life. By identifying your treasures, you can release items and activities that are no longer serving you. During this step in the process, keep in mind ways to recycle and donate your unwanted items. God's presence will allow you to see "all things new" within your space.

It is normal to hesitate and ask yourself while going through this step, "Who am I without all this stuff?" I have witnessed many people who so strongly identify with their stuff. They find it very difficult to let go because they believe their identity is contained in the stuff rather than in God. Stuff has power.

But now, God is calling us to have a new identity . . . one that is solely in Him. This new identity will connect you to Christ and not with your stuff.

Ask yourself, "Am I in love with God or just His stuff?"

As the Holy Spirit reveals this new truth to you, you will be able to part with the things from your past.

This process is easier when you know who'll get your castoffs: a charity, a shelter, or possibly your sister. Have boxes or shopping bags ready for each person or organization that is getting donations. There is a great difference between eliminating and organizing. First you must eliminate, then you can organize.

Step 2: Where do you begin in a room? (a review from chapter seven)

My favorite method to help determine where to begin in a room is to ask, "What area is bothering me the most?"

Have all the needed equipment with you in your "circle of work." Have your "keep," "trash," "donate," and "take-someplace-else" bins within arm's reach of the circle. Don't forget to label these bins. Choosing this one spot in the room will keep your focus on that area until everything is completed. The secret is to not move from that spot until everything has been uncovered and placed into the appropriate bin. Then move to either the left or the right and continue to sweep the entire room in a systematic process.

Distractions occur when we zigzag in our decluttering because we feel it is necessary to put things away immediately. In doing so, we forget what we were doing altogether. But when you have a take-someplace-else bin, those items will be put away at the end of your session.

You may feel that your room is so overwhelming you can't possibly know where to begin. The entire room is cluttered, and making that decision is very daunting. Here's a great tip to help you decide where to start. I have my clients get a paper towel roll and hold it over one eye, much like a telescope. I have them visualize everything that is within sight of the circle. Once they see the perimeter of the circle, they are able to focus on that small area. Moving from right to left using the roll helps them decide how much of the area they want to take on and how much time they want to spend in the room.

Whether you are looking to organize your kitchen junk drawer, your closet, or an entire room, the process is the same.

S.H.A.L.O.M.

Get Organized God's Way is taking you, the reader, on a journey to understand that true order and peace (shalom) are achieved through the knowledge of His organizing principles.

Shalom is a Hebrew word with many meanings that include peace, well-being, and wholeness. I find it interesting that "organizing" takes its root from the word "organic," which has the same root meaning that is whole, complete, one. I teach that organizing is not about our possessions, but the effect our possessions have on our life. When your space is well organized, there is shalom.

In a world filled with chaos, people are seeking peace and order that are within their control. This control usually begins with an attempt to organize a space. But attempts at organizing without the knowledge of God's order are futile. *Get Organized His Way* is taking you, the reader, on a journey to understand that true order and peace (shalom) are achieved through the knowledge of His organizing principles. Once His peace abides within our homes, our ability to hear His voice is magnified, our relationships become meaningful, our gifts and talents are defined, and our purpose on earth is clarified. Many books are designed to help

God is a God of order. Order is an expression of love, while disorder and chaos are destructive and separates us from God.

people get organized, but few books describe God's order . . . His way.

God is a God of order. Order is an expression of love, while disorder and chaos are destructive and separates us from God. Most Christians desire God's peace and order, but their physical environment and actions express just the opposite. Fear in one form or another prevents us from releasing the clutter from our lives.

Clutter in the home is a distracting force that keeps us from hearing and following God's design for our lives. *Get Organized His Way* is a blueprint to help you understand why God desires order in our lives. Once this information is received, realized, and applied, the skills to create and maintain this new order can become a lifestyle, which can then be passed down to future generations.

Here are the six steps to follow to achieve God's lasting S.H.A.L.O.M. in your life:

S: Sort

Take all the items in your drawer or in a small section of your closet or room out into a center sorting staging area. Begin to sort "like" things together. For example: If you're going through a junk drawer, separate pens, rubber bands, takeout menus, coupons, etc., and separate them into their respective piles. Once you see the kinds of items you have in your drawer, then you can begin to make decisions as to what items are of value (the ones you use all the time) and which items can be eliminated.

H: Heave

As you sort, seeing what you want to keep (items you use and those in good condition) and what you want to toss (items no longer needed or broken) will become obvious. This heaving process can be a two-step procedure.

1. Discard the obvious items.
2. Make decisions with the items you want to keep but are not currently using (those that are still in good shape or those that may be seasonal). For example: Do you need five ice-cream scoops in your kitchen drawer? Could you move four of the scoops still needed for that once-a-year ice-cream party to another area of the home for seasonal storage?

The bin method will help you to decide how best to sort items.

For example: In your dresser drawer, do you really need thirty pairs of black crew socks? Sometimes you can heave while you are sorting; and at other times, it's only after you have sorted that you can see just what you have. Then the heaving process becomes more obvious.

A: Assign a Home

Here is where most of my clients make their first mistake in the organizing process. Once they have determined what they will keep, the immediate reaction is to containerize the items. The next step in the organizing process is determining its location or home. If you have multiples of like items that need to be contained into one space, then you will need to contain them. But before you run out and buy that container, you need to measure the home it's going into.

For example: If you are putting pencils into a drawer, you need to measure the height of the drawer. If you buy a container that is two inches high and the drawer is only one and a half inches high, you've wasted your time and money. The item's home will determine the size and shape of the container. Always take your measuring tape with you when purchasing your containers. Make good use of your time and money by planning first and then purchasing appropriately sized containers.

Putting items in close proximity to where they are used will ensure that the items will be returned to their rightful containers. Organizing is a breeze once you know where the items will go.

L: Limit

It's important to limit the number of items in the home to prevent clutter from building up again. Consider implementing a "one in, one out" rule to keep things in check.

O: Organize for Optimization

Look for ways to optimize the use of space in the home. This can include using vertical storage, utilizing underbed and over-the-door organizers, and incorporating multipurpose furniture. Once your vision for the space is optimized, getting organized is easily realized.

M: Maintain

Just like any new habit, skill repetition will ensure lasting results. Maintaining means returning the item back to its home after you use it. Remember, new habits take time to establish, so don't worry if you slip up now and then. Just remember, you have already determined where something has to go. That is most of the battle.

Questions To Ask for Eliminating Excess

Clutter is the result of postponed decisions. It's not the know-how or answers that keep us from making those decisions; it's the questions that elude us. Here are a few of my tried-and-true questions to ask yourself as you go through the sorting and purging process.

1. Why have I been keeping this?

2. Have I used it in the last year?
3. Does it bring me joy?
4. Am I keeping this solely because I would feel guilty if I got rid of it?
5. If I have multiples of these, how many do I really need?
6. Is this a seasonal item that I can store elsewhere?
7. Am I tired of seeing it? Thinking about it? Cleaning it? Moving it around?
8. If I were not going to keep this, would someone else find it useful?
9. If I'm going to keep this, is there a better place for it?
10. If I need it again, can I get another one? Can I find it in the library or on the internet?
11. Is this item obsolete? Will it be obsolete by the time I want to use it?
12. What is the worst thing that would happen if I didn't have it?

Equipment for the Job

Having basic equipment with you before any organizing job begins is crucial for a successful session. Here are just a few of my essential tools to get the job done:

- Plastic totes for sorting
- Bins/baskets of varying sizes
- Label maker
- Marking pen (Sharpie, felt-tip marker)
- Timer
- Digital camera/cell phone for taking before and after pictures
- Tape measure
- Sticky notes
- Scissors
- File folders/hanging file folders
- Banker boxes
- Swiffer® duster
- Zip-top bags of all sizes

Before you begin your session, make sure everyone knows that *you are not to be disturbed*. Put pets in a separate area, let your voicemail pick up your calls, and concentrate for a set time (usually, thirty minutes is a good start).

After thirty minutes, take a break, go outside for some fresh air, drink water or eat, and then tackle the area for another thirty minutes.

With your full attention applied to the task, you will be more than amazed at what you can accomplish. I also find it helps to have music playing in the background. Whistling while you work really does turn work into play.

Just Do It!

Yes, organizing can be a dirty job, so before you begin, remember to wear loose clothing and keep a water bottle near you. There will be many mental and emotional decisions to make, as well as physical movement. Be sure there is ample lighting in the room.

Where to Start?

Have you noticed how your energy is zapped just walking into your home? Starting at your entry is a great way to remove the energy zappers from your home. Creating a clean, organized space at the entry truly says, "Welcome home."

Another place to begin is to ask yourself what bothers you the most, or what will give you the greatest satisfaction once the project is completed. Do you crave more family time? Is the kitchen in such disarray that it's difficult to cook a meal? Start there. The kitchen will nourish your body and your family's soul.

Is Aunt Martha coming for a two-week stay next month? How about starting in the spare bedroom to make her feel welcomed? If you have a time-sensitive need, that is also a great place to begin. So . . .

Let's Get Started

1. What area is bothering me the most?

_____

_____

2. What is my goal/vision for this project?

_____

_____

3. What questions do I need to ask myself in order to form a criterion for keeping and heaving?

_____

_____

4. How much time do I have to devote to this project?

_____

_____

5. What is the plan for the day?

_____

_____

6. Do I need help or assistance?

_____

_____

7. What supplies do I need?

_____

_____

Achieving Your Goals Little by Little

Setting goals and deadlines is a great way to keep on task with your organizing. First, decide how much time you can spend on organization in a normal week. If it's two hours, then identify the tasks that take approximately that much time.

Scenario: Thanksgiving is six months away. If you would like to have your home organized by the beginning of the holidays, then create a weekly or daily schedule that will allow you to accomplish your goals within the set amount of time. For example, your schedule for your kitchen might look like this:

1. Organize all-purpose drawers.
2. Organize lower cabinets.
3. Organize upper cabinets/plan seating arrangements.
4. Organize pantry/plan meals.

5. Clean refrigerator/freezer.
6. Create list of needed items to purchase (dishes, pots, pans, food, etc.).

Missing the planned activity because of unknown interruptions is okay. Padding your time for interruptions is essential to keep that overstressed feeling from creeping back. Having your list will help keep you on track.

Organizing, like any new activity, becomes easier with practice. Don't let the "perfect" be the enemy of the "good." If you find it hard to concentrate, work for only fifteen minutes at a time, then take a ten-minute break and go back for another fifteen minutes. Your break time will help you regroup and focus until the room is mentally functional.

Taking It to God

Father,

I understand that all things must be done decently and in order. My environment should reflect this order so that my mental, emotional, and spiritual life can become more in line with Your plan for my organized life. I have the knowledge to begin this lifestyle change, and now, Holy Spirit, I ask You to fill me so that my mind stays sharp, my body is protected from injury, and my spirit stays uplifted so that I can complete the work set before me.

Right now, the work seems like Mount Everest and an impossible task, but I know that, inch by inch, I will see progress. Help me to stay focused and encouraged when the going gets tough. Lord, I need You to give me the vision to see the areas that need changing, and the courage and strength to put in the effort necessary to change them. I will reflect on Philippians 4:13 (NLT), "For I can do everything through Christ, who gives me strength." Amen.

Chapter 12
What's in Your Closet?
Clothes Reflect Our Spiritual Identity

And they were both naked, the man and his wife, and were not ashamed. . . . And the serpent said unto the woman, Ye shall not surely die: for God doth know that in the day ye eat thereof, then your eyes shall be opened, and ye shall be as gods, knowing good and evil.

Genesis 2:25; 3:4–5 KJV

O nce upon a time, all was right on planet Earth, and Eve didn't notice her nakedness. Adam and Eve were in perfect communion with God and each other. They were naked, vulnerable, and completely okay with it. They were secure in themselves and who they were with God. Eve had no understanding or shame of body type or image.

I imagine that immediately after her first bite of the forbidden fruit, as her eyes opened to sin, her mind was flooded with thoughts something along the lines of:

Look at me . . . Oh my gosh, how did these get here? Okay, I have to go back to our tree and find something to cover up "the girls." I know! I'll go shopping for just the right leaf. Oak leaf . . . no . . . leaf too small. Pine needle . . . no . . . too itchy. Oh look, that fig leaf . . . smooth texture . . . right size, and oh . . . there's a maple . . . not bad either, which one . . . Hmm . . . Adam, which one? Do you like the fig or the maple? The fig leaf? You really like the fig? Oh brother, same boring green . . . guess it will have to do. I have nothing else to wear.

And the eyes of them both were opened, and they knew that they were naked; and they sewed fig leaves together, and made themselves aprons. (Genesis 3:7 KJV)

151

As new effects of sin entered the world, a new industry was birthed . . . fashion! Eve could never have foreseen the effect that her actions would have far into the future, nor the enslavement women would shoulder. From that moment on, women would find their identity through the clothes with which they covered their bodies. They would also desire a different body type so that others would find them more desirable. As quickly as women change their minds about what looks good, an increasingly dominant fashion industry bombards them, telling them that what looked good yesterday doesn't work today.

Adam and Eve saw that they were naked and decided they must cover themselves up. Isn't it typical that people think *their* self-sufficiency can cover up sin? The fig leaves that Adam and Eve chose to use to cover their nakedness were quickly replaced. God provided a covering for them with quality skins to replace the hasty and insufficient leaves they had made for themselves. When we try to cover our sin ourselves, it doesn't work. We may try to lie, ignore it, or cover it up somehow, but these tactics will not last. Leaves dry up and fade away, but animal skin . . . now you're talking—it's tough and durable. The symbolic fig leaf that man chose to use was quickly replaced by something God found redeemable for this act of rebellion. A lamb.

"The shedding of the blood of the lamb was a demonstration of the only means by which man could gain forgiveness [sin's covering]. This principle, established in the Garden, culminated in the sacrifice of the Messiah through whom redemption can only be achieved."[39] Talk about deep symbolism!

> But he was wounded for our transgressions, he was bruised for our iniquities: the chastisement of our peace was upon him; and with his stripes we are healed. All we like sheep have gone astray; we have turned every one to his own way; and the LORD hath laid on him the iniquity of us all. He was oppressed, and he was afflicted, yet he opened not his mouth: he is brought as a lamb to the slaughter, and as a sheep before her shearers is dumb, so he opened not his mouth. (Isaiah 53:5–7 KJV)

To Think About

So what's the point to all of this, and how does it relate to our closets today?

Clothing protects our bodies against the elements and is a basic need in every society. However, clothing can also express our inner beliefs about ourselves. For example, some use clothes as a way to cocoon and make themselves blend in because of a deep emotional trauma. For others, the closet represents an aura of status and superiority reflected in designer labels. The clothes closet is a direct indication of their values and their willingness to spend in order to be noticed.

A recent client couldn't wait for me to witness her closet. Her wardrobe was the main focus of our organizing session for the day; I could tell she was delighted that this was where we would be spending our time together.

Upon entering her closet, I couldn't help but noticing many designer shoes (some never worn) and many designer labels on her dresses and accessories. She seemed almost intoxicated by the fact that the closet reflected an aura of status few could rival.

The professional organizing industry is by nature a witness to what society values. Our western world hungers to be significant and is willing to do anything to obtain attention. Getting noticed and adored is the hallmark of all advertisements.

Jesus was very clear in His admonishment to the Pharisees in Matthew 23:1–7:

> Then Jesus said to the crowds and to his disciples: "The teachers of the law and the Pharisees sit in Moses' seat. So you must be careful to do everything they tell you. But do not do what they do, for they do not practice what they preach. They tie up heavy, cumbersome loads and put them on other people's shoulders, but they themselves are not willing to lift a finger to move them.
>
> "Everything they do is done for people to see: They make their phylacteries wide and the tassels on their garments long; they love the place of honor at banquets and the most important seats in the synagogues; they love to be greeted with respect in the marketplaces and to be called 'Rabbi' by others."

The status of a rabbi was reflected by their garments and intended to indicate their spiritual superiority. They sought to increase that impression of superiority by the design and placement of the phylacteries and tassels. It was of upmost importance that they project a superior "rabbi" attitude. This would ensure that they would gain respect and obtain all the very best places of honor. Their aim was to be noticed and revered.

Jimmy Choo shoes say much the same; at least, they spoke to my client that way. Her hunger for significance is an inherent drive that desires recognition and relational significance. Her attempt to find that significance through material possessions is common within our industry. We see it played out not only in material goods but in careers, vacation destinations, and friendships. As a professional organizer, I see the twisted intent of a world searching for significance without the Lord.

Your closet may hold a great many emotional thoughts and beliefs that no longer fit. I recently had a client who was extremely proud that she had saved every article of clothing from her college days. Each item of clothing represented a memory in time that she was unable to physically discard. Her closet was emotionally charged because she transferred her memories to items that reminded her of where she was at certain times in her life. Her closet had become an emotional museum. Event dresses held special meaning, pregnancy clothes reminded her of days before children, and plus and minus sizes reminded her of body types she couldn't control.

> *Your closet may hold a great many emotional thoughts and beliefs that no longer fit.*

However, she was continually frustrated in finding clothes she could actually use. As we change, grow, mature, and develop, we can look back and say, "That served me well at the time, but now I can let it go and move forward."

After a few sessions, my client was able to let many items that were in good condition go to a women's shelter. She began to understand that it's not a matter of "Do *I* need it," but "Does *it* need me?"

> *She began to understand that it's not a matter of "Do I need it," but "Does it need me?"*

Questions for Reflection:

1. What inner beliefs are you expressing about yourself through your clothes?

_____

_____

2. What things do you need to let go of now so you can move forward?

_____

_____

3. What steps can you take to bless others with the items no longer needed?

_____

_____

Lorry's Story

This one doesn't fit right. This one is worn out. Maybe someone else would like this item. This bargain was not such a bargain after all!

These were just some of the thoughts that went through my head as I cleaned out my closet. It's amazing how clothes collect and just hang there month after month, and some even year after year. My closet rods seemed to let out a sigh of relief as I lifted off the unnecessary weight they had been supporting. Now there was room for the remaining garments to hang freely and not be wedged in so tightly that they suffered wrinkles or creases.

As I looked at my closet, I thought about the "prayer closet" that each Christian has with the Lord. It's not a literal closet, but the place in our hearts where we can commune with Him. Sometimes it seems as if life is tightly packed with things that are not really valuable or may even be unfitting in our walk with the Lord. We may have allowed ourselves to buy into things that are not appropriate "garments" in our spiritual wardrobes. These items are dangerous because they can fill up our thoughts and time, cramping out space for the Lord.

It feels so good to get rid of unnecessary loads of compromise, frustration, anger, worry, pride, or whatever else we might have allowed the enemy to hang on us. Through prayer we can ask God to help us take inventory of our hearts and toss out anything that may be getting in the way of His presence. Without the needless clutter, everything fits well and feels good! Our prayer closets become more restful, peaceful, and comforting when there is plenty of space for the Lord to abide.

Has your prayer life felt hindered lately? Try cleaning out your prayer closet. It is a wonderful relief to get rid of the excess and make room for the Lord!

What's in Your Closet?

Step 1: Your Vision

Before diving into the closet, decide the vision for your space. Is the closet to remain a catchall for other homeless items in the home? Or are you now willing to devote this space to just the clothing items that you are currently using? The following vision steps will help get you started:

- Move items that don't belong or can be stored someplace else.

I have had many clients find past Christmas presents buried two feet deep in their closets. These were not opened presents; these were presents they either couldn't find or forgot to give away. What a waste of time and money!

But wait, that's not all. Their closets also became home to an array of sports equipment, kitchen appliances, and bathroom essentials. By relocating these items to their appropriate rooms, the closet can once again breathe. It's just amazing how this one step can put a smile on your face. Decide what types of items can stay and what goes within your vision.

- Take everything out of your closet you either don't want or you seldom wear.

Examples could be your formal attire, long-hanging items, or special winter (think bulky) clothing. It's critical that you do not place these items in an attic or garage. They must be kept in a well-ventilated room or else the fabric will deteriorate faster than the moths can eat.

One of my clients got her girlfriend to split the monthly cost of a climate-controlled storage unit. Now that's a friend! Your vision for the type of clothes and seasons may change during the year. Make sure your other closet spaces can adequately handle the overflow.

As stated earlier, we hang on to our clothes for a variety of reasons. However, hanging on to your stuff like the other clutter in your home prevents the creative spirit from coming alive. Once you truly love what's in your closet, getting dressed should be a fun and pleasant activity. Are you hanging on to beliefs and behaviors that no longer serve you? Are you ready to clean out your closet and make room for you?

Step 2: Practical Steps to Eliminate Items

Now that you have completed your vision steps, these next practical steps will help you eliminate excess from the closet.

- Don't keep it if it's too big or too small.

Take all of your clothing out of your closet and decide what fits. Donate the off sizes to someone who can wear them. Even if you're trying to lose or gain a few pounds, it's not worth keeping. Live in the *now*.

- Don't keep it if you don't like it.

This is a no-brainer. Get rid of it *today*.

- Don't keep it if it's stained.

If you *really* like the garment, but can't wear it because it's stained, prioritize time this week to get that stain washed out. If you can't get the stain out, take the garment to your local dry cleaner. If he can't get the stain out, and there's no other way for you to hide the stain, such as a patch or accessory, then bite the bullet and part with this piece of clothing.

- Don't keep it if it's torn.

A hem needs to be sewn or it needs to be taken in to fit. Either repair or discard the item if the price of the repair is not worth it. Make one of these choices today, rather than allowing this damaged item to take up precious space in your closet.

- Don't keep a wear-once outfit.

If you have a wedding dress, prom dress, or other wear-once dress in your closet, you have an emotional decision to make. If you can't bear to part with these items because they bring back happy memories, then you may have to just keep them.

However, if you have photographs of yourself in the wear-once outfit and that's good enough for you, consider parting with it so that someone else can make his or her own good memories in that outfit.

On the other hand, if they bring back bad memories, by all means get rid of them. Bring them to a consignment shop, sell them at your next garage sale, or donate them.

- Match your item.

Perhaps you have a shirt that you love, but can't seem to find pants to match it, or vice versa. Make it a point to go shopping in search of that perfect match. Remember, neutral colors such as black, brown, navy, beige, and gray go well with most other colors. You might even want to bring the piece you have to the store with you and have a sales clerk help you find a good match. Try a reputable department store so you can get professional assistance before you make your choice. You'll be thrilled that you can finally wear that shirt that's been hanging in your closet!

- It's all too much!

If your closet is packed with clothes and you have outfits you never wear simply because it's hard to see with so much crammed in a small space, you may want to consider putting some of those clothes into storage. If your budget allows you to invest in a closet system to better organize your closet, so much the better. Once your closet is organized, you will be able to see all the possibilities your clothing presents.

- Don't keep it just because it was expensive.

Have you ever splurged on a pair of shoes that blew your budget, only to realize that there was no way you could ever wear six-inch stiletto heels outside the house? Your purchase may have cost you a lot of money, but if you're not going to wear it then it's just taking up space in your closet. Toss it, or better yet, take it to a consignment store.

- Don't keep it because it was a gift.

Who hasn't received a well-intentioned clothing item that ended up being a dud? Don't we all have oversized sweaters or strange scarves that were given to us? Yes, you may feel guilty giving away an item that was a gift, but you're not wearing it anyway. Donate it to charity and perhaps it will find a second life with someone who will actually wear it.

For my fiftieth birthday, I told my husband I wanted a walk-in closet. I was tired of having everything scrunched together and not seeing the possibilities before me. After a good hard purging session and a beautiful walk-in remodel, I can now locate what I need when I need it. I can also coordinate according to my daily whims. (The inner fashionista in me has broken free.) I just love my closet because I feel good knowing what I have.

The same is true about my walk with God. God has given us a variety of talents and possibilities, but because we have scrunched up our lives with busyness, we can't see all the possibilities He created for us. Letting go and purging what is no longer serving us unlocks the creative power within us.

Our identity in Christ is wrapped in our outer garments. Don't believe me? Just take a good look at what you have on now. Like the caterpillar that sheds its chrysalis and becomes a new creature, shed your past closet identity of outgrown beliefs and behaviors, and let God work His amazing transforming power.

Closet Organization Tips:

No longer are my clients afraid of what might fall on their heads. They are relieved and joyful when they can finally access their closets' full potential.

Here are my top seven strategies and techniques that will have you singing instead of moaning when you enter the dark and mysterious space that was once your closet.

1. Start with a bright light.

   How can you see anything in the dark recesses of your closet unless you shed a little light on the subject? Using new LEDs or CFLs is the safest and most environmentally effective choice. Find the right light bulb for your closet area, remembering that they come in a range of colors from warm to cool.

2. Find more hanging space.

   If your clothes are crammed together like sardines in a can. No, you don't have to bump your son out of his room and make that your closet; all you need is to create a double hanging rod. Hanging rods that hook over existing rails are a smart, inexpensive, and an instant way to create extra room for short-hanging clothes. Look for products called "double hanging rods." (For example: Honey Can Do Chrome Adjustable Hanging Closet Rod

3. Consider a valet rod.

   When I was designing my own closet for my birthday present, I decided that putting in a valet rod was my best decision. A valet rod is a small pullout metal rod about 5–7 inches. The rod will allow you to temporarily hang an item and then push it back when you are finished using it. I use it every single day when I'm deciding what to wear the next day. I really have fun deciding what to match. I also use it to hang my dry cleaning on before it goes back into the correct section of the closet.

4. Count the number of empty hangers in your closet.

   Let's examine those free wire hangers you get from the dry cleaners. You say, "They're free, so why do I have to pay for expensive hangers?" There's a good reason why wire hangers are free; they're basically worthless. If you want to prolong the life of your clothes, don't keep them on wire or flimsy plastic hangers. Wooden, padded, or velvet hangers are the best ones to use for maintaining the shape of a garment.

5. Install hooks for your scarves and/or belts.

    This is another organizing wonder. Until I installed my belt hook, my belts and scarves invariably got tangled up or lost on the floor. These also work well for ties.

6. Create more space for shoes.

    A shoe rod that is a shorter version of the traditional hanging shoe bag will fit in a double-hanging-rod system. Another nifty trick is to make use of the back of your closet door with an ingenious rack that can hold up to twelve pairs of shoes along with other accessories.

7. Use clear shoeboxes.

    They are not just for shoes! This smart organizing container is great for sorting bras, underwear, socks, and hosiery.

Going through these simple tips will only take fifteen minutes a week, will result in a better wardrobe system, and enhance the way you perceive yourself. You are worth it!

Taking It to God

Father,

You say that when I pray, I am to go to my closet, shut the door, and pray in secret so that when I pray, I am concentrating only on You. Right now, if I go to my closet, I'm afraid the only thing that could get in is my left foot. I have crammed so much unwanted and unneeded junk in there that there's no room for me, let alone You, God. It seems that my closet has been a metaphor for my life. I am continually cramming my life to overflowing, without filling my heart with the most important things—time with You and the eternal things that come from You.

My closet represents who I was and who I presumed to be, putting my identity in my outer garments and not in Christ Jesus. Father, as I begin to shed the superficial outer garments of my life, I pray that Your Holy Spirit will come in and fill me, clothing me in Your righteousness. Help my life to reflect what is most important, focusing on the eternal and not the material.

Thank You that You are always ready to help me start anew and move forward. I commit all of this to You, asking that You will help me to be ever aware of the things that take my focus off You. May the closet both in my heart and in my home glorify You. Amen.

Chapter 13
Organizing with the Sword: Detecting, Diagnosing, and Dealing with Spiritual Environments

Do not bring a detestable thing into your house or you, like it, will be set apart for destruction. Regard it as vile and utterly detest it, for it is set apart for destruction.

Deuteronomy 7:26

Since we have these promises, beloved, let us cleanse ourselves from every defilement of body and spirit, bringing holiness to completion in the fear of God.

2 Corinthians 7:1 ESV

I have titled this chapter "Organizing with the Sword" because when we begin to organize, we must tear down the false beliefs that have held us captive to our lifestyle of excess and possession control.

The sword that I refer to is the same sword Paul used to describe in Ephesians 6:17, the "sword of the Spirit." Paul sees that we, the Church, have been given a weapon that is meant to rip our enemies to oblivion. This sword, taken from the word "rhema" illustrates the Word of God. Rhema is a word that is spoken vividly when believers understand the unmistakable, unquestionable, definite terms of what is spoken to us. This word seeps into our very existence and becomes a part of us.

As you have been organizing your spaces, perhaps you have encountered many rhema moments. I certainly pray you have. Now we must use our sword to divide and conquer those ideas and things that hold us back from complete deliverance from the clutter. We must "cleanse" inside and out.

Before my professional organizer days, I was called to help with what is known as "spiritual house-cleansing." Spiritual house-cleansing takes its roots from the Old Testament. In fact, in 2 Chronicles 29:16 it says:

> The priests went into the sanctuary of the LORD to purify it. They brought out to the courtyard of the LORD's temple everything unclean that they found in the temple of the LORD. The Levites took it and carried it out to the Kidron Valley.

Fast-forward to our modern purification. In Eddie and Alice Smith's book *Spiritual Housecleaning*, they state, "God is calling us to a new level of holiness. We need to cleanse the atmosphere of our homes as well as our hearts. This cleansing often involves the removal of certain physical possessions."[40]

> *"God is calling us to a new level of holiness. We need to cleanse the atmosphere of our homes as well as our hearts. This cleansing often involves the removal of certain physical possessions."*

In the many spiritual house-cleansing sessions that I have been called into, it is interesting to note that these homes had a very displeasing atmosphere. Something didn't feel right. I didn't just wake up one day feeling led or equipped to become involved in this type of ministry. I had spent many hours researching this topic, sitting under various teachers, and drawing from my own pre-Christian experiences. After several years of study, I understood the process for dealing with unclean objects. But even *after* the cleansing was completed, it became increasingly clear that there was a common denominator in many of these homes . . . disorganization.

Being raised in a Jewish home, I was given complete access into what is referred to as Jewish mysticism—the Kabbalah. I spent hours speaking with Kabbalah teachers and rabbis, growing in the knowledge of numerology and hidden meanings. This knowledge of Kabbalah gave me a firm foundation that things are not always what appears on the surface. These teachers never used the word "demonic" to express these teachings.

From Wikipedia, the free online encyclopedia, the definition of "occult" is:

> The *occult* (from the Latin word occultus "clandestine, hidden, secret") is "knowledge of the hidden." In common English usage, "occult" refers to

"knowledge of the paranormal," as opposed to "knowledge of the measurable," usually referred to as "science." The term is sometimes taken to mean knowledge that "is meant only for certain people" or that "must be kept hidden," but for most practicing occultists, it is simply the study of a deeper spiritual reality that extends beyond pure reason and the physical sciences.[41]

Before I knew that an industry of Professional Organizers existed, I sensed a strong correlation between a cluttered environment and a person's beliefs. The previous chapters have illustrated this in detail. In this chapter, we'll take it a step further.

It's not *only* our beliefs that cause clutter buildup. Unholy objects brought into the home can become contributors to this as well. For some of you, this will seem strange, but it's possible to have certain objects or items in your home that create an accursed (meaning "under a curse") atmosphere. Accursed items can cause confusion, arguments, and a chaotic environment within the home.

> *Accursed items can cause confusion, arguments, and a chaotic environment within the home.*

In Perry Stone's book, *Purging Your House, Pruning Your Family Tree*, he says:

If the angelic world is moved toward us by prayer and praise and worship and can identify the exact locations of ancient altars and blood sacrifices, then the kingdom of darkness is also moved by our words and attitudes and can be attracted to certain objects we bring into our lives or homes.[42]

Going through your home and examining your possessions periodically is a very healthy activity. During your SHALOM-ing and organizing process, you may have encountered several questionable objects. Maybe in the back of your mind you had questions about keeping them. When we cleanse our homes spiritually, we need to look for things that might defile our homes by providing an opening for demonic activity. You may now have many questions regarding these objects, and this chapter is a great way to begin seeking some answers.

More Than an Organizer

Not long ago, I had a wonderful client who wanted to organize his home. We started with the kitchen, then the living room, and then we moved upstairs to the office. Every time I entered the office, I felt queasy and unable to focus. Because I am aware that unholy objects sometimes generate this reaction, I am very up-front with my clients when I begin to notice this sensation.

I told my client that sometimes, when I begin to feel unfocused, there might be something in the room that may need to be placed elsewhere.

He looked at me and said, "I guess when I hired you as an organizer, I got a lot more than I expected."

We both laughed.

As we began to declutter and remove months of piled papers, I uncovered a crystal ball. I never judge my clients. Instead of saying, "This must be the cause," I asked my client to tell me about the object.

He said that while on vacation in New Orleans, he had purchased the crystal ball in a voodoo store. Need I say more?

I never tell my client that he or she must trash anything. As part of my education on spiritual house-cleansing, I learned that the owner, as legal guardian of the object, must decide the fate of his item. My position is to make the client aware of certain conditions and to offer encouragement and instruction—if he asks for it. At the same time, I must come against anything that stands in the way of the mission to which God has called me.

I calmly asked my client if we could move the ball into a different room. He complied.

Upon his return into the office, he stopped. He took a deep breath and said, "Wow, I never realized how bad all this clutter was making me feel. It's as if a veil has been lifted, and now I can see this office for the first time. I now realize that I just felt so lethargic and confused whenever I came in here."

He asked me if there was a correlation between the crystal ball and the way he was now feeling.

I redirected the question back to him and said, "What do you think?"

He said that I had given him a lot to think about. This was the opening for me to share my beliefs, since he now respected my position.

What Does It Mean to Cleanse Your House Spiritually?

I am convinced that there is a great need to educate the Christian community regarding the importance of the spiritual cleansing of our homes. By now you understand the physical and emotional connection that clutter weighs on your mind and body, but God specifically states that we are a triune being. 1 Thessalonians 5:23 says:

May God himself, the God of peace, sanctify you through and through. May your whole spirit, soul, and body be kept blameless at the coming of our Lord Jesus Christ.

It's interesting to note that when a space is physically (bodily) in order, our emotions (soul) become calmer and our minds (soul) are much more focused to the task at hand. When organizing your home, it is vital to always keep in mind the *spiritual* aspect and ask God if there is anything accursed in your home. The Word of God teaches us the value of things unseen and the invisible dimension of life.

If you are unsure about whether to remove some items from your home, ask God and obey the leading of the Holy Spirit no matter what the cost. You may not fully understand the prompting of the Spirit of God, but once you obey, His revelation will come.

To Think About

Acts 19:19–20 (AMPC) says, "And many of those who had practiced curious, magical arts collected their books and [throwing them, book after book, on the pile] burned them in the sight of everybody. When they counted the value of them, they found it amounted to 50,000 pieces of silver (about $9,300). Thus, the Word of the Lord [concerning the attainment through Christ of eternal salvation in the kingdom of God] grew *and* spread *and* intensified, prevailing mightily."

How can God bless our homes when we have items that dishonor Him?

Ephesians 5:8–11 says:

For you were once darkness, but now you are light in the Lord. Live as children of light (for the fruit of the light consists in all goodness, righteousness and truth) and find out what pleases the Lord. Have nothing to do with the fruitless deeds of darkness, but rather expose them.

Although the Scriptures may not explicitly say, "Behind every idol is a demon," the principle is clearly taught in Scripture.

Read 1 Corinthians 10:19–22.

What are your thoughts?

_____

_____

First Things First

Every room in the home needs to be inspected, even the attic and basement and the outside surrounding areas. If you are curious about a certain object, the first question to ask is: "Does this glorify God?"

The following is a list of items that will need your attention and prayer:

- Much of what we bring home from vacations is rooted in pagan religious ceremonies. If there are items of superstition, even if handed down from previous generations, they can give a foothold to the demonic, so they need to go.
- Obviously, anything demonic, such as posters, T-shirts, videos, spirit games, items of astrology, tarot cards, charms, amulets, or any other thing having to do with witchcraft must be burned or discarded.
- Any item that represents other religions such as Buddhism, Hinduism, ancient Egyptian gods, Freemasonry, and symbols of fertility has no place in a Christian home.
- Pornographic material has no place in a Christian home. (This includes magazines, TV, or computer access.)
- Children's toys, video collections, and games may have something of the occult nature in them.
- Jewelry given or bought that denotes the same connotations needs to be dealt with as well.

When dealing with such items, they must *not* be given away. They need to be destroyed, discarded, or burned so no one else can use them.

Organizational Tips: Spiritually House-Cleansing Your Home

There are two helpful ways for spiritually house-cleansing your home: purging and prayer.

Purging Your Home:

1. Remove.

    Begin at your foundation of the home. This can be in your basement or under the home. Go through every area, storage box, etc., to examine each object to make sure it is not offensive to God. You may be surprised by what you find in your treasures!

2. Repent.

   Repent of each item and the sentimental value it has had over your life. The very fact that you have kept the item suggests a strong emotional bond. Remember, the only person who can discard an unholy item is you! If the owner is deceased, but you brought it into your home as a remembrance, it is now considered yours.

3. Restore.

   Restore the home with a fresh atmosphere through prayer. God loves new things. The Bible speaks of God doing a new thing (see Isaiah 43:19). God said that we would have a new heart and a new spirit, and become a new creation. Don't be afraid of losing your old things. God will give you exceedingly more!

Prayer Of Cleansing for the Home:

It's important to cleanse your home from demonic strongholds and pray through every room of the house. Here is a sample prayer from Dr. Preston Bailey to guide you:

By the blood of Jesus Christ, we now address every demonic spirit who is on this land and property, in this home and belongings, on and around people and pets, and tell you to leave immediately, go in the name of Jesus Christ. I renounce and reject any inch of this house and property that has been yielded or surrendered to Satan, and by faith I take it back and surrender it to the Lord Jesus Christ. By faith, I claim that this room is under the blood of the Lord Jesus Christ and no evil spirit can enter it. Father, we ask for forgiveness for any sins or activities committed in this home and land that enabled the enemy access to this home, land, and its people. We cancel all authority given to Satan by previous owners or tenants, and we break all access points, curses, contracts, legal agreements, and holds in the name of Jesus Christ. Amen.

After going through every room in the house, pray:

Father, I dedicate and consecrate this home to the Lord Jesus Christ. I surrender everything in this house to the Lord Jesus Christ and claim it is under His divine protection, including all electrical wiring and plumbing. I bind every evil spirit that is in this house by the precious blood of the Lamb, and command them to flee and go where the Lord Jesus Christ sends them. I claim, by faith, that everything in this house is covered by the blood of Jesus Christ from the top of the roof to the bottom of the footing.

We ask You to cover each area, every nook and cranny, with the blood of Jesus. We pray blessings and anoint every room and possession in the name of Jesus Christ.

I claim by faith that this house is surrounded by a hedge of protection, a wall of fire, a wall of faith, covered under the blood of the Lord Jesus Christ on all sides, above, and below. I pray that powerful warring angels would come to protect the four corners of this house and property and everyone inside. Thank You for the complete victory we already have in Jesus Christ. I ask that this home be consecrated with Your divine presence so that everyone who enters it will be blessed with spiritual blessings from heavenly places.

I bless this place in the name of my Lord and Savior, Jesus Christ. Amen.[43]

It's Not Mine!

Suppose you are living with a roommate who has demonic posters on the walls, or perhaps you have a family member who has possessions that you now understand dishonor and displease God. What do you do? Understand that you do *not* have the right to destroy or remove someone else's property. Pray first. Ask God to give you favor before speaking to the person, and above all else, go to them in love. Your request should be very well thought out and prepared. Don't base your discussions and opinions on superstition, but have with you scripture that explains your position. Above all else, ask God for direction and the timing of the encounter and always go with gentleness and respect.

In completing my research for this book, when reading Eddie and Alice Smith's book *Spiritual Housecleaning,* the following words jumped off the page:

> Just so, the Church today is crippled because Christ's people are overlooking a necessary key that unlocks the door to revival—to rid ourselves of corrupt things. Are there accursed things in your home? Deuteronomy 7:25–26 warns us that objects of idolatry, even silver or gold, could ensnare us.[44]

Let me be perfectly clear. Spiritual house-cleaning is *not* about superstition, paranoia, or legalism. Understanding God's heart and becoming sensitive to His leading will help you make the right decisions with regard to your possessions in your home. Having a home that pleases God and establishes an atmosphere of joy and peace will be one to which others will naturally be attracted. Light in a home will illuminate the darkness, and where there is light, darkness *must* flee.

Having a home that pleases God and establishes an atmosphere of joy and peace will be one to which others will naturally be attracted. Light in a home will illuminate the darkness, and where there is light, darkness must flee.

For Further Reading:

1. *Spiritual Housecleaning: Protect Your Home and Family from Spiritual Pollution* by Eddie and Alice Smith
2. *Ridding your Home of Spiritual Darkness* by Chuck Pierce and Rebecca Wagner Sytsema
3. *Purging your House, Pruning your Family Tree* by Perry Stone

Barbara's Story

This chapter really surprised me. The house we live in was built for us; no one had ever lived in it before. We had discarded many things before we moved in and prayed God's blessing on our new home.

So it was unexpected when I sensed the Holy Spirit reminding me of a box in my bedroom closet. It contained an album of my mother's wake, which was created by my aunt, her sister who does this for all family members. I've had it for ten years but had never opened it. I thought I might want to see it someday, but not now.

This scripture from Matthew 22:32 came to me. Jesus was speaking about what God said, "I am the God of Abraham, the God of Isaac, and the God of Jacob," and explained, "He is not the God of the dead, but of the living."

I felt Him telling me that there is nothing of my mother in that box. She is alive in heaven with Him. I had not even thought about the album until I cleaned out my closet. I didn't open it but put it back on a shelf in my newly cleaned-out closet. That was four days ago.

Today in the chapter on "Organizing with the Sword", He is telling me to let it go. I am amazed, first at how gentle His words and thoughts are to me and how clearly I am hearing His voice. Then, how easy it is for me to let it go, because I know it's what He wants for me. So I took the box and put it in the garbage can for pickup the next day. When I came back into my bedroom, there was something different, which I can only describe as lightness, and I could feel it.

This world and what is in it is a shadow of what is real, what is in heaven. God is there, and it is His home. Yet because I am a believer, He makes His home in me. He is so patient and kind. He wants my home to be a reflection of Him and His ways. He loves order and peace. He delights in showing mercy. He is preparing a place for me in heaven, but He has also prepared a place for me here and now. He sees it completed and pleasing to Him. He has started me on a lifelong journey of living His way in the home that He has provided for me. He has opened a new door in our relationship, and it overwhelms me and brings me to tears.

Thank You, Lord God, for Your unfailing love. Thank You for never giving up on me.

Taking It to God

Lord,

Thank You for this opportunity to glorify You in my home. I put all my hope and trust in You, for I believe You alone have power and authority in heaven and on earth. I have no authority, no power, no strength, and no dominion of my own, for everything I have or do is through Jesus Christ who gives me strength. I now come to You, asking for a total cleansing of this place so that this place will glorify You, Lord Jesus. Holy Spirit, I trust You to do this work right now. I claim this place to be filled with Christian spiritual safety and protection. I renounce any sinful items ever kept here. Father, I ask You to bring to my mind any item that does not glorify You. If anyone has ever entered this place that put a curse either knowingly or unknowingly, I renounce these curses now in the name of Jesus. Amen.

Chapter 14
More Stuff than the Stuff: Generational Causes of Clutter

The LORD, the LORD, a God merciful and gracious, slow to anger, and abounding in steadfast love and faithfulness, keeping steadfast love for thousands, forgiving iniquity and transgression and sin, but who will by no means clear the guilty, visiting the iniquity of the fathers on the children and the children's children, to the third and the fourth generation.

Exodus 34:6–7 ESV

In the two decades plus that I have spent as a Certified Professional Organizer, I have come to have a greater understanding that Chronic Disorganization (CD) can, in many cases, be generational. As stated, "An Idol Called Clutter," the Institute for Challenging Disorganization (ICD) (www.challengingdisorganization.org), defines Chronic Disorganization as "having a past history of disorganization in which self-help efforts to change have failed; an undermining of current quality of life due to disorganization; and the expectation of future disorganization."

What the ICD organization definition doesn't include is that most people suffering from CD (like the majority of my chronically disorganized clients) have had a family member with the same condition. It's easy to see how this could happen and why this "normal" living condition would be at their comfort level, but I believe it runs much deeper than this.

For CD clients who are also Christians, there is a deeper emotional and spiritual entanglement regarding their stuff. As stated by Sheila Delson, CPO-CD, CVPO, cofounder of ICD:

Because we are spiritual people having a human experience, I've learned that when it comes to clutter management and control, there are two main elements that can affect its outcome. Those two elements are a physical (home) environment and a person's individual beliefs. Many times both are the product of inheritance . . . for better or worse!

Your belief system and your home are two strongholds that have an impact on decision-making abilities and your ability to follow through. If either one of those two elements represents negativity, then both become intertwined—an amalgamation of emotional entanglements, resulting in confusion, procrastination, and stagnation. In many CD cases, there is a direct correlation between our inheritance (genetic and/or our environmental) and our living conditions. [I would add that there is also a strong spiritual component linked to our outer behaviors.] The healthier your emotions, the easier the process is for "healthy" decision making in the organizing process. The opposite is true of unhealthy emotions, and both results are predictable.[45]

Does God have anything to say to us regarding this?

The LORD passed before him and proclaimed, "The LORD, the LORD, a God merciful and gracious, slow to anger, and abounding in steadfast love and faithfulness, keeping steadfast love for thousands, forgiving iniquity and transgression and sin, but who will by no means clear the guilty, visiting the iniquity of the fathers on the children and the children's children, to the third and the fourth generation." (Exodus 34:6–7 ESV)

Connie's Story

One day I woke up with the thought that this isn't normal. I can't remember how old I was, maybe four or five. It seemed to me that my mom couldn't take care of the house, so the task was left to me and my brother, but we were only five and eight and not very good at it. My grandmother would come over and before long, she'd argue with my mom about taking us away. The house seemed very much the same as my aunt's house.

Now that I think back, many of my mom's family lived with a great amount of disorganization, but not my grandmother. I never knew my grandfather, so I'm curious if this was something he passed down to his children.

This reminded me of the scripture in Numbers about the sins of the fathers visiting to the third and fourth generations.

As a daughter in Christ, my eyes are now open, and as God continues to open my heart and eyes, the clutter is going! I'm not in need of acquiring to feel accepted. I'm not feeling the need to surround myself with stuff to shut out others. God is certainly doing a marvelous work. It's funny; as I declutter, I can understand His Word so much better! God is so good!

The reasons behind the thinking and action behaviors in CD clients are extremely complex and must be dealt with by a professional.

Kristina is a fifty-seven-year-young recovering hoarder. She lived with animal feces, cardboard boxes stacked to the ceiling, and barely a path to move on in her two-story one-bedroom Nashville townhouse. A retired professional, Kristina lived as a hoarder for twenty-plus years. She informed me that both of her parents were hoarders, as is her brother.

Kristina is honest and transparent, and made the decision to transform her lifestyle to one that is organized and functional. To date, her home has been completely cleaned up, mold remediation has been conducted, structural repairs have been completed, and she is renovating her home!

Kristina is grateful for her "new life" and has told me numerous times that there is no more darkness, only the Son is shining in! Of course, that reminds me of the chapter on "Let God Shine His Face upon You." Thankfully, we are blessed to share God's love, and she has found a new life in Christ. Her "donation trips" to a local church become her "Blessing Days" for the underserved community in which the church is located. Kristina now attends church on a regular basis with her son and his family—praising God with an "attitude of gratitude" that she was given another chance to live *free*!

Here is the how and why.

Kristina was motivated to finally face and transform her hoarding disorder and confront the need in her home by a desire to open her home to others and have a safe space for her grandchildren to visit.

The grandmother made the decision to begin decluttering and solicited the help of a professional organizer. But not just any organizer would do. She insisted on finding one that held a deep underlying knowledge of how her clutter walk was interfering with the walk God had planned for her, and one that could answer a long-held deep belief that had bothered her since childhood. Noticing that hoarding was a problem for her grandparents and her parents as well, Kristina observed she came from a family of hoarders. Many psychologists believe that this could explain why she has also been stricken by the disorder.

Compulsive Hoarding and Heredity

Studies have shown that those with compulsive hoarding have at least one first-degree relative with hoarding problems, suggesting that hoarding is hereditary. In one study, over 50 percent of compulsive hoarders had a first-degree relative with similar hoarding problems. A large study based on twins found that genetic factors accounted for 50 percent of the variance in hoarding behavior, with environmental factors making up the other 50 percent.[46]

Jessica Brody states on Crosswalk.com:

There are things that do seem to carry from one generation to another. Beyond family traits such as skin, hair, and eye color, there are other things, like mental illness or alcohol and drug addiction, that pass from parent to child and beyond.

Science indicates there are certain genetic predispositions that carry from family member to family member, not to mention things such as abuse or a penchant for anger or gambling that are environmental influences.

But these are consequences and genes, not curses. While our genetics might make us predisposed to cancer, addiction, or depression, that is not necessarily our destiny or our own doing.[47]

One might assume after reading the above testimonies that everyone that grows up in a hoarding or Chronically Disorganized household would have the same traits. Heaven forbid, no! Not everyone (thank goodness) picks up these traits or habits even if their childhood experiences are inflicted with parental dysfunctions. However, if one does show these traits or tendencies, many Professional Organizers—myself included—have witnessed profound similarities within the family structure. That is why I felt it necessary to write this chapter. However, I want to make it very clear that it does not represent everyone with these early environmental issues.

Adopting the mental attitude that "I don't own it—it owns me," and facing the truth about this statement, will force many to finally embrace a new belief to become free. No longer running away from the root issues, coupled with the forgiveness of those that fostered this trait, is a powerful first step.

Cynthia's Story

I find that the clutter gets in the way of so many things—specifically, being able to focus on schoolwork, devotions, and spiritual growth; the ability to get my finances in control; and to find things when I need them. (I lose things I want so often!) But maybe this should be more motivation to get rid of the things I'm not sure if I will use again.

Sometimes I plan to return items but lose the receipt or the items. I've been thinking about why I have such a problem with clutter—I think the fact that I grew up around it is influential. My mom had an especially hard time throwing anything away. My grandmother (her mom) has stories of having roaches and animals around.

The mess gives me more control in not having people in my room. I'm sure God can speak to me and reveal why I feel so bitter and confused regarding my family. I have been in several counseling sessions at church, but no one really can help me dive deep into these generational issues and why this runs so much deeper than even I can see in the natural. I know this is a deep spiritual battle, but my church just doesn't seem to understand or is so ill equipped to deal with this issue.

I know I am not alone in this, as I have talked to several other members at church and they also are dealing with different levels of clutter and disorganization in their lives. So why on earth has the church not addressed this issue? In light of the many Bible references and the seemingly abundant materialistic nature our Western world has so mindlessly adopted, it is a bit perplexing that this topic has not made it into church studies. Our church could do more to help Christians, especially those of us in wealthy, developed countries, to get at the spiritual roots of having too much stuff—and at the effects it has on our planet.

What seems to be a common thread throughout both Cynthia's and Kristina's families is the level of trauma that each experienced in some way. These trauma issues also contributed to the hoarding, and both knew they were not alone in this understanding.

All hoarding begins with trauma, but the deepest traumas connect with us on our spiritual level, that which is at the very root of our being. If we don't address the underlying trauma in the people that hoard, it continues to impact them negatively. And most importantly, *it can impact people for generations to come.*

Can you relate to either of these testimonies?

_____

_____

Can you write down your story?

_____

_____

Breaking the Bondage of Generational Sin

> And God spoke all these words: "I am the Lord your God, who brought you out of Egypt, out of the land of slavery. You shall have no other gods before me. You shall not make for yourself an image in the form of anything in heaven above or on the earth beneath or in the waters below. You shall not bow down to them or worship them; for I, the Lord your God, am a jealous God, punishing the children for the sin of the parents to the third and fourth generation of those who hate me, but showing love to a thousand generations of those who love me and keep my commandments. (Exodus 20:1–6)

A vital step in obtaining your freedom in Christ is to renounce (to refuse to follow, obey, or recognize any further) the sins of your family. The iniquities of one generation can adversely affect future generations unless the sins of the ancestors are acknowledged and renounced and your spiritual heritage in Christ is claimed.

You are not guilty for the sin of your ancestors, but because of their sin, you may be predisposed to certain strengths or weaknesses and influenced by the physical and spiritual atmosphere in which you were raised. These conditions can contribute to causing someone to struggle with a particular sin.

To assist you in this powerful process of prayer and discovery, ask the Lord to show you specifically what sins are characteristic of your family. There is great peace and purpose in saying—in choosing—not to carry the stuff from previous generations anymore.

Hallelujah!

> Jesus replied, "Very truly I tell you, everyone who sins is a slave to sin. Now a slave has no permanent place in the family, but a son belongs to it forever. So if the Son sets you free, you will be free indeed." (John 8:34–36)

The apostle Paul offers these encouraging words in his letter to the Romans:

> For just as through the disobedience of the one man the many were made sinners, so also through the obedience of the one man the many will be made righteous. (Romans 5:19)

We are "set free from sin" through our faith in Christ (see Romans 6:20–22). Hoarding had its roots deep even in biblical days (see King Hezekiah's Hoarder Intervention[48]):

When Hezekiah became king over Judah, God's house could almost have been compared to any home that is severely in need of order. The interior of the temple was trashed.

One of the first things Hezekiah did was open the doors of the temple. And the Levites began to take out the trash. First, they cleaned up the temple. Then they began to clean up their nation. You see, just as God's temple had been cluttered with junk, the people of Judah had filled their lives with garbage. They had adopted the sinful ways of the surrounding nations. And their lives were full of filthiness. Taken from the spiritual root; the natural is always led by the spiritual nature of a people.

Because of their immorality, the people faced eviction from their land and condemnation by God. So when Hezekiah came to power, he launched a nationwide intervention to clean things up.

This amazing renewal initiated by King Hezekiah is recorded in 2 Chronicles 29:4–6 (ESV):

> He [Hezekiah] brought in the priests and the Levites . . . and said to them, "Hear me, Levites! Now sanctify yourselves, sanctify the *house of the Lord* God of your fathers, and carry out the rubbish from the holy place. For our fathers have *trespassed and done evil* in the eyes of the Lord our God; they

have forsaken Him, have turned their faces away from the dwelling place of the Lord, and turned their backs on Him" (emphasis added).

Notice how God's temple is referred to as the "house of the Lord" in the Old Testament. Now consider God's house under the New Covenant.

The Temple of God Under the New Covenant

Do you not know that you are the temple of God and that the Spirit of God dwells in you? (1 Corinthians 3:16)

The apostle Paul calls each one of God's people His temple!

A person's dwelling place is a person's home. The temple is where God's Spirit dwells. So if you have God's Spirit dwelling in you, that makes you God's temple and also His house.

If anyone defiles [pollutes or makes unclean] the temple of God, God will destroy him. For the temple of God is holy, which temple you are. (1 Corinthians 3:17 NKJV)

Are You Keeping Your Spiritual House Clean?

Do you recognize that your most valuable belonging is having a clean spiritual life where God's Spirit can dwell? Or are you so consumed by the worthless things of this world that you fill this house—your heart and mind—with junk? (See 2 Chronicles 36:14–16 and Nehemiah 10:39.)

To God, you are worth so much more than the sinful junk of this world. That is why Jesus Christ came and died for your sins. He died so that your life could be cleaned out and become a fitting home for God's Spirit to dwell. (See 1 Peter 1:18–19)

In 2 Corinthians Paul once again calls God's people the temple of God. He shows how God's Spirit must live in a temple that is clean. Like oil and water, God's Spirit and sin simply don't mix.

For what fellowship has righteousness with lawlessness? And what communion has light with darkness? . . . And what agreement has the temple of God with idols? For you are the temple of the living God . . . Therefore, having these promises, beloved, let us cleanse ourselves from all filthiness of the flesh and spirit, perfecting holiness in the fear of God. (2 Corinthians 6:14b, 16a; 7:1 NKJV)

Follow King Hezekiah's example, recognize the value of God's temple, and clean it out. When it comes to the sinful pulls of life, always remember that you are worth more than this.

Breaking Generational Curses (from Globalchristians.org)

"Therefore, if anyone is in Christ, he is a new creation. The old has passed away; behold, the new has come." (2 Corinthians 5:17 ESV)

Jesus has broken every curse on the cross. So by His blood I now understand that my dysfunctional inheritance from my early family no longer controls my thoughts. My heavenly Father has washed me clean like snow, from the very cells in my body to the thoughts in my head. Father, I give you all glory for releasing me from the curse of my family's past sins and that I am no longer bound. I announce to the kingdom of darkness that your influence in my life and my family's life has ended. No longer will the lust after material goods become my obsession, but I will take every thought captive and be reminded that God supplies all that I need. I will trust in your provision and seek out the blessings you have for me daily. Your praise will always be on my lips and in my heart. In Jesus's name, Amen.

Taking it to God

Father,

By the blood of Christ, I now realize that my heavenly Father has not passed down this dysfunctional inheritance from my earthly generational family. My heavenly Father has washed me cleaner than snow, and no longer am I afflicted with these past generational strongholds. I am a new creature in Christ and that creature has been remade from the inside out.

My newness even reaches into my very genetic material. Father, I praise You continually that I do have a choice to be set free. I do have a choice to no longer continue in the ways of my earthly inheritance, but to put on a new garment of praise and live a life that You have ordained since the beginning of time. Free from the distractions of stuff, of competitiveness, anger, and low self-esteem.

Father, I give you all glory in restoring me to Your heavenly family and in Jesus's name, I will set aside time in my day to set free the constraints that have tied me to my stuff that suffocates my very being. I announce now to all demonic presences that their time has ended. I will no longer look at my objects as if they are a person, as if I am my stuff, and as if only they can bring me joy. Only You, Holy Spirit, can fill the empty places that will bring Your shining presence into this darkness. In Jesus's name, Amen!

Chapter 15
Pressing Toward the Goal: Proven Methods to Maintain Your Organization

No, dear brothers and sisters, I have not achieved it, but I focus on this one thing: Forgetting the past and looking forward to what lies ahead, I press on to reach the end of the race and receive the heavenly prize for which God, through Christ Jesus, is calling us.

Philippians 3:13–14 NLT

Learning to Maintain Your Organization

In the previous fourteen chapters, you have been saturated with how to change your mindset with regard to your disorganization, and you have been provided with the tools and strategies to get organized. Getting organized is not the problem at this point; *staying* organized is! This lesson is pivotal if there is ever going to be a lasting behavior change.

Hopefully by now, you understand that an organized space is not the final purpose. A space that will allow you to reach your "kingdom" purpose is your ultimate goal. Your kingdom purposes will be achieved because hearing God's voice in a calm and peaceful

---

Your kingdom purposes will be achieved because hearing God's voice in a calm and peaceful environment will propel you onto the road He has purposed for you. Keep praying, keep moving, and keep imagining what your goals and priorities are for your home.

---

environment will propel you onto the road He has purposed for you. Keep praying, keep moving, and keep imagining what your goals and priorities are for your home.

Terminology of House and Home

A house denotes a transitory dwelling; a home implies a sense of ownership and responsibility. How you envision your dwelling will either have the clutter creeping back in, or it will motivate you to maintain its organized state. Taking ownership and thinking through everything brought into your home will keep the wild beasts at bay. In the *Wizard of Oz*, Dorothy said it best: "There's no place like home."

A peaceful home is as sacred a place as any chapel or cathedral. —Bill Keane, creator of the "Family Circus" comic strip.[49]

Shelly's Story

Sometimes, in the middle of the night, I would wake up in a panic in case anyone should come over the next day. Then I started praying every night before I fell asleep. I asked God to show me one thing He wanted me to do with the house the next day. I would plan it in my mind, see it successful, and go to sleep with a happy thought. When I am intentional to give these panic issues to the Lord, to ask Him how He wants to take care of it, I gain control. No longer do I feel overwhelmed. Sometimes the chore is a trifling thing, like taking the garbage out or changing the sheets. At other times, it is something that will take more effort. But since He is the one who gave me the job, I know I can get it done!

What Does Your Kitchen Say?

The kitchen is more than cooking central. Your kitchen is truly the heart of your home. The kitchen is where family relationships grow and where your important decisions are made. A kitchen says so much about your family and their priorities. It can be especially revealing to look at all the little sayings on the refrigerator and walls.

One of the first activities I do with my clients is to have them look at all the sayings they have in their kitchen. For example:

- "Behind every successful woman is a sink full of dirty dishes."

- "I clean my house every other day. This is not the other day."
- "Housework is un bear-able." (On a sign with a teddy bear.)
- "I hate housework."

These visual plaques send the opposite message for the desired organized kitchen. I offer up a new saying, "Magnify the Lord, Minimize the Mess!"

Maintaining is not a one-time get-it-all-organized event; rather, maintaining is the diligence to do it over and over and *over* again. These new habits form a new lifestyle, and soon this new lifestyle is part of your daily routine.

Maintaining means forming new habits, and habits begin with your thought processes. You can choose to listen to the negative messages hanging in your kitchen, or have positive thoughts and visions of a nourishing kitchen.

Scripture Study

For all the negative thoughts you say to yourself, God has a positive answer.

You say: "It's impossible."
God says: "All things are possible." (Matthew 19:26)

You say: "I'm too tired."
God says: "I will give you rest." (Matthew 11:28)

You say: "Nobody really loves me."
God says: "I love you." (John 3:16)

You say: "I can't go on."
God says: "My grace is sufficient." (2 Corinthians 12:9)

You say: "I can't figure things out."
God says: "I will direct your steps." (Proverbs 3:5–6)

You say: "I can't do it."
God says: "You can do all things through Christ." (Philippians 4:13)

You say: "I'm not able."
God says: "I AM able." (2 Corinthians 9:8)

You say: "I can't forgive myself"
God says: "I forgive you." (1 John 1:9; Romans 8:1)

You say: "I can't manage"
God says: "I will supply all your needs." (Philippians 4:19)

You say: "I'm afraid."
God says: "I have not given you a spirit of fear but one of love, power and self-control." (2 Timothy 1:7)

You say: "I'm always worried and frustrated."
God says: "Cast all your cares on [Me]." (1 Peter 5:7)

You say: "I don't have enough faith."
God says: "I've given everyone a measure of faith." (Romans 12:3)

You say: "I'm not smart enough."
God says: "I give you wisdom." (James 1:5)

You say: "I feel all alone."
God says: "I will never leave you nor forsake you." (Hebrews 13:5 NKJV)

God's words to Joshua as he entered the Promised Land are meant for all of us. Joshua 1:7 says:

> Be strong and very courageous. Be careful to obey all the law my servant Moses gave you; do not turn from it to the right or to the left, that you may be successful wherever you go.

This Scripture tells us never to fail to obey God's Word. Don't turn aside in any way. Oh, how easy it is to get distracted! However, this time you have resolved not to let things return to disorder. Maintaining takes diligence and commitment, and in the previous chapters, you have been given the tools to succeed.

What Does God Say about Diligence?

Read through the following verses and write down what they say about diligence.

Philippians 3:14

_____

_____

1 Corinthians 9:24–25

_____

_____

2 Timothy 2:4–6

_____

_____

Ecclesiastes 9:10

_____

_____

1 Thessalonians 4:11–12

_____

_____

The discipline of diligence can bring many blessings into your life. Committing to getting your home and life organized takes resolve and a well-thought-out plan. God will bless your efforts as His plan for your life becomes clearer every day. Organizing is not a quick fix, no matter how many how-to books would have you believe it is. My prayer is that while you are in the midst of this process you don't lose your resolve, moving on to something else that is easier and perhaps more appealing. Take a cue from God's Word to Joshua. Stay on the path you committed to until you are fully successful!

The Roots of Clutter

There are literally thousands of wonderful organizing how-to books on the market, and finding one that speaks to your personality is not so very hard to do. What is hard to find is any information that will get to the root issues of why the clutter is there in the first place. Why do we have our piles in certain locations and what do those piles say about us? In symbolic terms, each room or area of your home carries special significance, and where clutter resides may reflect a spiritual component of your life. Let's begin by dividing up the home into rooms, and let me take you on a journey to expose your roots of clutter.

Clutter in the Kitchen

We have all heard the saying, "The kitchen is the heart of the home." More than cooking central and a place of nourishment, the kitchen is where we sort through our feelings and interpersonal conflicts, and get clear on priorities. When the kitchen is cramped with clutter, it makes it hard to nourish anyone, on either the physical or spiritual level.

Decluttering your kitchen opens up space for you to receive the support and comfort that you need in life. When the kitchen fosters that kind of support, not only can life decisions be made with clarity and confidence, but also there is a marked increase in nourishment, both in terms of nutrition and relationships.

Clutter in the Bathroom

Never underestimate your health and the bathroom. The bathroom contains past health reminders, from bandages to expired medications. Your bathroom can and should become a room filled with refreshment and renewal. A cluttered bathroom makes it impossible to find the peace and quiet as we start each day. Clearing the clutter from your bathroom will not only open you to those great aha moments in the shower, but will start your mornings with renewed energy and vitality.

Clutter in Attics and Basements

Many people have a just-in-case storage facility in their basement. A wide variety of activities can be associated with them. It's where we store things we have not yet made sense of but might need someday. Our basement, or the foundation of our lives, becomes jumbled and confusing when there are piles and cartons representing old pursuits (e.g., college books and manuscripts) and past dreams. When there is so much of the past in our foundation, our future purpose can be put on hold.

Before you put something else in the basement or the other storage areas of the home, ask yourself these questions:

1. Do I love it?
2. Do I need it now?
3. Can I see someone in my family loving or needing it in the next year?
4. What's the worst thing that could happen if I didn't have it?

Decluttering the basement frees you to let go of useless items, and at the same time, allows you the choice of future possibilities. How about that hobby or start-up company you've been putting off?

Clutter in the Bedroom

The alpha and omega . . . the bedroom is the first and the last place in our daily life. How we begin our day depends on how well rested we are, and our rest depends on the environment of the bedroom.

The bedroom reflects areas in our lives that are particularly private. When a bedroom is cluttered with items or activities not associated with rest, such as a desk piled high with paper or a television show depicting violence and anger, these items and activities can present issues that could have a negative effect on both rest and intimacy.

Clearing the bedroom clutter will give you greater rest and deeper dreams. Clients report a deeper prayer life when they pray in a clutter-free bedroom.

Clutter in the Hallways

Like the veins in your body, the hallways represent the arteries of your home. For many families, the hallways are areas that accumulate the most visible clutter, from shoes, toys, and laundry. Your home can be very well organized in other rooms, but the hallways are filled with constant clutter. How well you move from room to room depends on the traffic tie-up in the halls. Do you store pieces of furniture there that you have to maneuver to get around? Are the kids' toys spilling over into the hallways? Is an accident just waiting to happen there?

We all know what happens if our arteries are clogged on the way to the heart. The same thing happens when hallways are jammed with clutter. Frustration abounds, and eventually, your health is going to suffer.

Clutter in the Family Room

Whether you are watching TV with your family, engaging in games, or conversing with friends, the time spent within this room can produce lasting memories, especially during holidays and celebrations. Clutter can turn these social spaces into dens of isolation, especially if the clutter prevents you from inviting people into your home. A peace-filled family room produces many fun-filled hours of relationship building.

Clutter in the Home Office

Last, but certainly not least, is the home office. Desk clutter can prove to be physically and mentally overwhelming. Not only is it bill-paying central, but also the desk represents mission control for your life.

Does your paper control you, or do you control your paper? If clutter reigns in your office, fresh and inventive ideas are pushed aside. When your office area is streamlined to reflect your goals and priorities, letting go of the excess becomes clear.

Organizing Tips: Seven Common Mistakes in Organization Maintenance

1. The burst of enthusiasm.

    Usually the "burst of enthusiasm" begins when you see wonderful organizing products. You buy first and organize later. It's the fifteen-minute excitement of digging deep and then seeing the effects of the "bomb" in the room. Discouragement, paralysis, and depression deepen with each passing minute. The problem: You didn't develop a plan before digging in. The area is now far worse than the beginning. Tears follow. Before you begin, ask yourself:

    - What is the desired outcome or goal?
    - What are the steps to achieve this goal?
    - What is my motivation to change?

2. Unrealistic time expectations.

    In other words, how long will this take? Time is very elusive and different for each of us. What takes one person an hour to organize can take another person fifteen minutes and another person three hours. It depends on your mood, focus, and decision making, and how into "organizing" you are. Always plan for more time than you need so when there are interruptions, your motivation will still stay high. If you end sooner than expected, so much the better!

3. Doing an incomplete job.

    Remember that postponed decisions equal clutter. Sorting and purging are both physically and mentally challenging. Tough decisions, both emotionally and intellectually, are constantly being made, as well as a lot of climbing, stretching, and reaching. Most people give up 50 to 80 percent of the way through completion because they are just too tired to continue. Remember to keep hydrated. I find it very calming to have praise music in the background.

4. Keeping more than you have space for.

    Many people are unrealistic about how much can be stuffed into their rooms, closets, and drawers. By now, you have experienced that space is a good thing and that a room needs to breathe in order to keep it a calm space. Take your sock drawer as an example. If you have fifty-plus pairs of black-and-white socks—all organized, but stuffed into a drawer—I can guarantee you it won't take more than a week for the drawer to end up in chaos again. Get rid of unnecessary possessions, give your space room to breathe, and it will stay organized.

5. "But that cost me good money!"

    Saving unused items just because you spent good money on them is another common mistake. For example: The expensive suit or sewing machine you bought. I know that discarding expensive items feels like throwing money down the drain, but keep in mind how much they're costing you in cluttered spaces and frustration. Give yourself permission to release your mistake purchases. Remember, someone else could really use that item, and God is waiting for you to bless others with it. One way to recoup is to take your expensive items to a consignment store, Craigslist, or eBay. There are many clothing resale apps (e.g., liketwice.com).

6. Inconvenient storage.

    How many times have you not put things away because cleaning up is too much of an ordeal? Storing items too far away from where you use them is called "inconvenient storage." When you store items too far away from where you actually use them—across the hall, in another room, or at the opposite end of the house—it requires a big trip to put things away. For example: You don't put your books away and they continue to pile up next to your reading chair because your library is upstairs or down the hallway. Or perhaps your drawers stick and are almost impossible to open, or the cabinet is broken. Other hindrances could be boxes and furniture that block your closets. Your storage bins are stacked too deep, or your shelves are too high to reach. The bottom line is: if it's too hard to put something away, you simply won't do it. But once you have established a home for your items where you use them, it's easy to put them back where they came from.

7. Taking your space for granted.

Sometimes we take our homes for granted. Take the time to appreciate your home. If you really love your environment, you'll be more inclined to care for it. It might seem obvious, but at times we forget what we have in our lives.

For Reflection

- It's okay to be imperfect.

Don't expect your habits to change overnight. It takes time. Sure, there will be days when you're sick, or life's demands will simply get in the way, but remember that even in the worst-case scenario, getting back on track will be much easier than starting over.

- Associate with positive role models.

Spend time with people who model the habits you want to mirror. Proverbs 12:26 says, "The righteous choose their friends carefully, but the way of the wicked leads them astray." First Corinthians 15:33 says, "Do not be misled: 'Bad company corrupts good character.'" Associate with people who reflect godly character and values.

These associations can occur on two levels: (a) *active engagement*, where you inform your friends who might be interested in your goals and cultivate the habit together with them or (b) *passive engagement*, where you let others know about your plans and have them morally support you. As you continue on your journey, attracting people into your life with these skills will help you maintain your newly formed habits. One day you will walk into your kitchen and not even remember the way it used to be.

1. Can you name some people in your life right now who model habits you want to mirror?

_____

_____

2. If you're not associating with people who reflect godly character and values, what are you doing to make changes in the company you keep?

_____

_____

3. Pray that God will help you maintain your newly formed habits, encouraged by the company you keep.

_____

_____

4. Pray that God will bring encouraging people into your life to mentor and help you become all God wants you to be.

_____

_____

At this point in the study, you may have made several attempts to organize by yourself. Or maybe you have asked your spouse or family members to join you, but the process has either come to a standstill and you just can't muster the strength to continue, or the scope of the work is simply bigger than you originally anticipated. You may feel like your ship is sinking, but I can assure you there is help available.

As a Certified Professional Organizer, I would advise you to consider contacting a professional organizer in your area. Professional organizers provide information, products, and assistance. A professional organizer will guide, encourage, and educate you about the basic principles of organizing by offering support, focus, and direction. The National Association of Productivity and Organizing Professionals (NAPO) offers organizers opportunities to sharpen their skills through ongoing education and professional development, and it has a code of ethics by which members are expected to abide. A professional organizer who is an NAPO member has made a commitment to his or her business and thus to you, the client. You can find an organizer near you through NAPO's online referral system at www.napo.net.

But wait—there's more help available.

My first NAPO annual convention was in 2004. At the beginning of our session each day, a handful of Christian organizers would gather in rooms to pray for the day, our leaders, and the conference. In 2006, this same group (myself included) decided to formalize. We called ourselves Faithful Organizers. It has been the mission of Faithful Organizers to provide community encouragement and networking opportunities for Christian Professional Organizers and to help clients find Christian Professional Organizers in their areas. If you are interested in seeking out a Christian Professional Organizer, our site (www.faithfulorganizers.com) would be the place to find one.

> *Where we spend our time, with whom we associate, and even the purchases we make will profoundly affect our vision of eternity.*

The Challenge

In the beginning, the Lord fashioned the universe in order. This study has been dedicated to helping you find order in your life and presenting God's Word and its practical application into your daily life. If you say you trust God but continue to have mounds of paper piles with little room to write or sit, then you need to reexamine that trust.

If you organize for organizing sake, you have missed the point of this workbook. Our life here on earth is so brief. If our life on earth was all we had, there would be no eternity. Each of us was made to live in the light of eternity, but realizing this impacts our relationships, our tasks, our circumstances, and our life's purpose. Where we spend our time, with whom we associate, and even the purchases we make will profoundly affect our vision of eternity.

> Every action in our lives touches on some chord that will vibrate in eternity.
> —Edwin Hubbell Chapin, American Clergyman (1814–1880)[50]

You have been on a journey as you have worked your way through this workbook. It's a journey and challenge to discover God's purpose and best for your life. An orderly life is one that will help you manage the stresses of life with greater faith and with greater joy. The day will come when you will meet Christ face-to-face. It's my sincere desire that you will hear:

> His master replied, 'Well done, good and faithful servant! You have been faithful with a few things; I will put you in charge of many things. Come and share your master's happiness!' (Matthew 25:23)

As you continue on this organizing journey, peace will continue to rule over your thoughts and spaces in your home and life. What are the practical changes you can make to restore divine order to other areas of your life that you have neglected?

_____

_____

Isabelle's Story

Discipline and diligence are so important. I can't change in one day what has taken years to build up. But as God leads me, I can be consistent and purposeful each day. I can decide to make my bed every day and keep my countertops cleaned off. I can decide not to let my old ways come back and to maintain what has begun to take place. I actually enjoy looking at my closets, which are now beautiful to me. I know, too, that order is starting to appear behind closed doors and cabinets.

I think of the scriptures, "He also brought me out into a spacious place; He delivered me because He delighted in me . . . You prepare a table before me in the presence of my enemies; You anoint my head with oil; my cup runs over." I am starting to have a vision of what my entire home will be like as I continue this lifelong process.

The Lord has a plan for me. He has everything set up. I have to see it, to walk through it, trusting Him. When I do, I'll find myself at the table He has prepared for me. A table beautifully set by Him in a spacious place, where I will find peace and calm. And I know that He made a way for me to get to the table because He loves me.

Lord, You amaze me. You take me places deep into You. I know Your love and forgiveness. Your Holy Spirit is in my life. You are God who created human beings and stars and universes. You have revealed your spiritual truths to me. And yet, You are concerned with every facet of my life, from the largest to the smallest. You are interested even in my closets and drawers. You are conforming me to Your image and as You do, my image of me will be left behind. I will run the race to receive the prize, which is You. Because of Your care in everything I do, You will enable me to live a life that will be pleasing to You. Thank You, Lord, for Your amazing love. Thank You that I have organized Your way.

Taking It to God

Father,

I know You love me and have wonderful plans for me. But sometimes I am overwhelmed by the thought of my future. I never want to return to the chaos again. Show me how to walk forward one day at a time.

May my heart be open while I search Your Word and listen to encouragement from others. By doing these things, may I hear Your call to live an orderly life that will let me love as only I can. Allow me to serve others with the special gifts You have given me. Purify my heart and keep my focus on You. Help me pursue You only, not turning to the right hand nor the left. Help me. Guide me. Lead me on!

"But one thing I do: Forgetting what is behind and straining toward what is ahead, I press on toward the goal to win the prize for which God has called me heavenward in Christ Jesus" (Philippians 3:13b–14). Amen.

About the Author

Eileen Koff CPO® is the owner and president of To the Next Level (www.tothenextlevel. net), a certified professional organizing business based in Cary, North Carolina, and Eileen Koff Ministries. (www.eileenkoffministries.com)

Ever since her teenage years, Eileen has taken great joy in helping people organize and simplify their surroundings. In 1998, Eileen was watching the *Oprah* show. Oprah's guest was Julie Morgenstern, a member of the National Association of Productivity and Organizing Professionals (NAPO). After listening to Julie describe her passion and business, Eileen realized that what she had been doing for free all her life was now a niche business. It took her five seconds to call NAPO and become a member.

Eileen received the industry's distinction as a Certified Professional Organizer (CPO) in the inaugural offering in 2007. She has served NAPO as their newsletter editor, communication project head for the education committee, course developer, and as Publication Chair from 2009 to 2013. She has also earned a level two certification as a member of the ICD (Institute for Challenging Disorganization). Eileen also served as Faithful Organizers' Education and Devotion Director, an international organization with Christian Professional Organizers in the US, Canada, and Australia. In 2011, Eileen became a columnist for *Just Between Us,* a Christian women's magazine.

To the Next Level became the first company in the professional organizing industry to receive an eco-consultant certification through Green Irene, a New York–based company specializing in promoting green awareness. Eileen was then appointed practice leader for other professional organizers incorporating green services into their business models. She was the featured eco-speaker at the NAPO 2010 conference in Columbus, Ohio, and was awarded "Best Green Service" at the NAPO-LA gala in 2013.

In 2012, Eileen wrote and developed a twelve-week Bible course called "Organize His Way" and taught her inaugural class at Smithtown Gospel Tabernacle.

Her passion is speaking and teaching various groups on the joys of leading an orderly life, but her obsession lies in witnessing the transforming power of God's Word in the lives of those she serves.

Eileen and her husband, Wayne, married forty-plus years, have three sons, and are now blessed with three daughters (in-law). When not organizing, she can be found enjoying the joys of cooking, traveling with her husband across the globe, continuing her passion for her foundation, Peace Island Children's Center (PICC) in Uganda (Peaceislandcc.org), and growing closer day by day to Jesus.

We are eager to hear from you.

Please send your comments about this workbook/study to the email address below. To book Eileen Koff, CPO, to speak for your event, call or write to:

EileenKoff@gmail.com

631-553-0068

Acknowledgments

Writing this study has been on my to-do list for many, many years. In 2004, I joined Sandra Felton's "Faith in Organizing" Yahoo group. My purpose as an organizer was to get a first-person perspective on how clutter and Chronic Disorganization interferes with the body of Christ. What I found from the numerous emails from this group exceeded my expectations. Those emails touched a deep desire in my heart to bring God's Word into Christians' lives so that true transformation could occur in their homes and in their relationships. You will read many of these women's testimonies in this workbook/study. It is my sincere prayer that you will no longer feel alone as you relate to their stories and struggles. I am so grateful to Sandra for having the vision to start this group, specifically for believers.

Writing this study would not have been possible without the help of Shelly Esser, editor of *Just Between Us* magazine. As she began editing this workbook/study, her encouragement gave me renewed confidence that it was truly unique and greatly needed.

My deepest gratitude goes to my husband, Wayne, and sons, Ian, Evan, and Keenan, for their patience, love, encouragement, help, and all the extra hugs as they encouraged me on this journey as an author. Thank you for sharing this incredible adventure with me.

After the study first came out in 2013 under the title *Organize His Way*, many of those whom I had taught and many of my fellow teachers saw the need to expand the content and update the book. I pray that God continues to bless this study, that He is glorified, and that lives are transformed for His kingdom.

Endnotes

1. Dotty Schmitt, *Stand on My Shoulders:Treasure from the Secret Places of His Heart* (Maitland, FL: Xulon Press, 2012), 71–72.

2. Bob Gass, "Get a Preparation Perspective," February 18, 2020.

3. Warren M. Marcus, *The Priestly Prayer of the Blessing: The Ancient Secret of the Only Prayer in the Bible Written by God Himself* (Lake Mary, FL: Charisma House, 2018) 164–165

4. Matthew Henry, *Concise Commentary on the Whole Bible* (Chicago, IL: Moody Press, 1983), 682.

5. David Cain, "I Don't Want Stuff Anymore, Only Things," Raptitude (blog post), January 19, 2011, https://www.raptitude.com/?s=I+don%27t+want+stuff+anymore.

6. Peter Walsh, interview by Eileen Koff CPO®, NAPO News, Dec 2008–Jan 2009, 1.

7. Rick Warren, *The Purpose Driven Life: What on Earth Am I Here For?* (Grand Rapids, MI: Zondervan, 2002), 44–45.

8. Brook Noel, "Are You Wasting Your Time and Energy?" (blog post), April 13, 2007, https://brooknoel.typepad.com/brooknoel/2007/04/are_you_wasting.html.

9. For more on this study, visit the Science 2.0 website, accessed by April 13, 2013, http://www.science20.com/news_releases/study_butterfy_memory_can_recall_uglier_caterpillar_days.

10. Rick Renner, *Dressed to Kill: A Biblical Approach to Spiritual Warfare and Armor* (Tulsa, OK: Teach all Nations, a division of Rick Renner Ministries,1991) 236–237.

11. Freya Stark, *The Journey's Eco: Selections from Freya Stark* (New York: Harcourt Brace & World, 1964) 161.

12. Eliezer ben Hurcanus, quoted in Leonard Swidler, *Women in Judaism: The Status of Women in Formative Judaism* (Lanham, MD: Scarecrow Press, 1976), 93.

13. Eliezer ben Hurcanus, quoted in James B. Hurley, *Man and Woman in Biblical Perspective* (Grand Rapids, MI: Zondervan, 1981), 72.

14. Flavius Josephus, *Jewish Antiquities*, trans. by William Whiston (Hertfordshire, England: Wordsworth Classics, 1997), 158.

15. Erica Brown, "Orthodox Judaism Grapples with Bat Mitzvah," My Jewish Learning (blog post), n.d., https://www.myjewishlearning.com/article/orthodox-judaism-grapples-with-bat-mitzvah/.

16. Dallas Willard, *The Divine Conspiracy: Rediscovering Our Hidden Life In God* (San Francisco: Harper, 1998), 212–13.

17. Claire Josefine, "Organizing as a Spiritual Art" (blog post), 2009, http://www.clairejosefine.com/art.htm#SABO.

18. Pam Pierce, "Understanding Simplicity," in *The Rewards of Simplicity: A Practical and Spiritual Approach*, ed. Pam Pierce and Chuck D. Pierce (Grand Rapids, MI: Chosen Books, 2010), n.p.

19. Walsh interview, 1.

20. Richard J. Foster, *Freedom of Simplicity: Finding Harmony in a Complex World* (San Francisco: Harper, 2005), 5–6.

21. Mac Hammond, *Simplify Your Life: Divine Insights to Uncomplicated Living* (Broken Arrow, OK: Word and Spirit Resources, 2010), 1.

22. Kevin Belmonte, *The Quotable Chesterton: The Wit and Wisdom of G.K. Chesterton* (Nashville, TN: Thomas Nelson, 2011).

23. David Henry Thoreau, *Walden: An Annotated Edition*, ed. Walter Harding (New York: Houghton Mifflin, 1995), 314. The quote used here is the common paraphrased version; the original is, "if one advances confidently in the direction of his dreams, and endeavors to live the life which he has imagined, he will meet with a success unexpected in common hours . . . in proportion as he simplifies his life, the laws of the universe will appear less complex, and solitude will not be solitude, nor poverty.

24. Henry David Thoreau, https://www.goodreads.com/quotes/8105541-go-confidently-in-the-direction-of-your-dreams-live-the.

25. E. F. Schumacher, "Small Is Beautiful," *The Radical Humanist* Vol. 37 No. 5 (1973), 22.

26. Wesley Zinn, July 29, 2009, *Courage and Vulnerability* (untitled blog post), http://wesleyzinn.blogspot.com/2009/07/.

27. Zinn, *Courage and Vulnerability.*

28. "Necklaces and Joyce Meyer," *Hickmama* (blog post), July 9, 2012, http://hickmama.blogspot.com/2012/07/necklaces-and-joyce-meyer.html.

29. Timothy Keller, *Counterfeit Gods: The Empty Promises of Money, Sex, and Power, and the Only Hope That Matters* (New York: Penguin Books, 2009).

30. Learn more on their website at https://www.challengingdisorganization.org/.

31. "Frequently Asked Questions for the Public" Institute for Challenging Disorganization, accessed April 13, 2013, https://www.challengingdisorganization.org/faqs..

32. Ariane Benefit, "The Truth about Chronic Disorganization: What Causes It and How to Heal the Trauma of Lifelong Overwhelm and Frustration" (blog post), October 19, 2011, https://web.archive.org/web/20111122061416/http://arianebenefit.com/blog/2011/10/19/truth-about-chronic-disorganization-understanding-what-causes-chronic-disorganization-and-how-to-heal-the-trauma-of-lifelong-disorganization-overwhelm-and-frustration/.

33. Peter Walsh, *It's All Too Much: An Easy Plan for Living a Richer Life with Less Stuff* (New York: Free Press, 2007), 6.

34. Glynnis Whitwer, *I Used to Be So Organized: Help for Reclaiming Order and Peace* (Abilene, TX: Leafwood, 2011), 81.

35. "Time Management for the Chronically Disorganized" (FS-005), Reprinted with permission from the Institute for Challenging Disorganization.

36. Judith Kolberg, *What Every Organizer Needs to Know About Chronic Disorganization* (Decatur, GA: Squall Press, 2008), 32.

37. Oswald Chambers, *My Utmost for His Highest* (Grand Rapids, MI: Our Daily Bread Publishing, 2017), https://utmost.org/don%E2%80%99t-plan-without-god/.

38. Joel Barker, "The Power of Vision" (training video), 1990.

39. "The Fig Tree," *Consider* (blog post), May 12, 2007, http://biblefocus.net/consider/v15FigTree/Adam_and_Eve_and_the_Fig_Leaf.html.

40. Eddie and Alice Smith, *Spiritual Housecleaning: Protect Your Home and Family from Spiritual Pollution, Revised and Updated* (Ventura, CA: Regal, 2009), 13.

41. Wikipedia, "Occult," https://en.wikipedia.org/wiki/Occult, accessed July 8, 2022.

42. Perry Stone, *Purging Your House, Pruning Your Family Tree* (Lake Mary, FL: Charisma, 2011), 19.

43. Preston T. Bailey, Jr., *Spiritual Warfare: Defeating the Forces of Darkness* (Camarillo, CA: Xulon Press, 2008), 147–148.

44. Smith and Smith, *Spiritual Housecleaning*, 101..

45. Sheila Delson, email to author, May 2011.

46. Renee Deveney, ed., "Is Hoarding Genetic?", https://www.therecoveryvillage.com/mental-health/hoarding/is-hoarding-genetic/, May 26, 2022.

47. Jessica Brodie, "Are Generational Curses Real Today?" Crosswalk.com, October 6, 2020, https://www.crosswalk.com/faith/bible-study/are-generational-curses-real-today.html.

48. Kris Kobernat, "Hoarders: Buried Alive," Life, Hope & Truth, November, 2015, https://lifehopeandtruth.com/change/sin/hoarders-buried-alive/.

49. Bil Keane, quoted in Brook Noel, *Good Morning: 365 Positive Ways to Start Your Day* (Naperville, IL: Sourcebooks, 2008), 402.

50. Edwin Hubbell Chapin, *Duties of Young Men*, Revised, 9th edition (Boston, MA: Putnam and Brother, 1856), 160; the quote used here is the common paraphrased version; the original is, "These deeds that are taking around you touch upon chords that extend by a thousand connections, visible and invisible, and vibrate in eternity."

ORDER INFORMATION

REDEMPTION PRESS

To order additional copies of this book, please visit
www.redemption-press.com.
Also available at Amazon, Christian bookstores,
and Barnes and Noble.

Printed in the USA
CPSIA information can be obtained
at www.ICGtesting.com
LVHW080738271023
762071LV00013B/473